Mini Musings

Miniature Thoughts on
Theatre and Poetry

ESSENTIAL ESSAYS SERIES 75

Canada Council   Conseil des Arts
for the Arts   du Canada

ONTARIO ARTS COUNCIL
CONSEIL DES ARTS DE L'ONTARIO
an Ontario government agency
un organisme du gouvernement de l'Ontario

Canadä

Guernica Editions Inc. acknowledges the support of the Canada Council
for the Arts and the Ontario Arts Council. The Ontario Arts Council
is an agency of the Government of Ontario.

We acknowledge the financial support of the Government of Canada.

Mini Musings

Miniature Thoughts on Theatre and Poetry

Keith Garebian

**GUERNICA
EDITIONS**
TORONTO · CHICAGO · BUFFALO · LANCASTER (U.K.)
2020

Michael Mirolla, editor
David Moratto, cover and interior design
Guernica Editions Inc.
287 Templemead Drive, Hamilton (ON), Canada L8W 2W4
2250 Military Road, Tonawanda, N.Y. 14150-6000 U.S.A.
www.guernicaeditions.com

Distributors:
Independent Publishers Group (IPG)
600 North Pulaski Road, Chicago IL 60624
University of Toronto Press Distribution,
5201 Dufferin Street, Toronto (ON), Canada M3H 5T8
Gazelle Book Services, White Cross Mills
High Town, Lancaster LA1 4XS U.K.

First edition.
Printed in Canada.

Legal Deposit—Third Quarter
Library of Congress Catalog Card Number: 2019949210
Library and Archives Canada Cataloguing in Publication
Title: Mini musings : (miniature thoughts on theatre and poetry) /
Keith Garebian.
Names: Garebian, Keith, author.
Series: Essential essays series ; 75.
Description: Series statement: Essential essays series ; 75
Identifiers: Canadiana (print) 20190180625 | Canadiana (ebook)
20190180641 | ISBN 9781771835343 (softcover) | ISBN
9781771835350 (EPUB) | ISBN 9781771835367 (Kindle)
Subjects: LCSH: Drama—History and criticism. | LCSH: Theater. |
LCSH: Poetry—Criticism and interpretation.
Classification: LCC PN1721 .G37 2020 | DDC 792/.09—dc23

for Don Mills
and his championship of my writing
and
for Rose and David Scollard
who have striven for the noblest promotion
of Canadian poets, especially of new voices

Contents

Poetry

Preface

In 2014, American playwright Sarah Ruhl brought out a collection entitled *100 Essays I Don't Have Time to Write*, in which (as its back cover boasted) "chimpanzees, Chekhov, and child care are equally at home." In examining the possibilities of the theatre, Ruhl engaged with subjects ranging from the most personal to the most encompassing issues of art and culture—all these becoming a map of her artistic sensibility and an existential guide, perhaps, for anyone who chooses the life of the artist. Umbrellas, sword fights, parades, dogs, fire alarms, children, chimpanzees, Chekhov, Calvino, Miller, Williams, Kushner, male orgasm, lice, Greek masks, Bell's palsy, motherhood, and so on were all part of her mix. Some of the pieces were a few lines long. One essay was exactly a single word. Most ran to a page. The longest ones spanned three pages.

One of Ruhl's epigraphs for the collection was drawn from poet Louise Glück: "I wanted to make something. I wanted to finish my own sentences." In my own case, I sometimes want others to finish some of my sentences, taking my opening gambits as launch-pads or provocations or motives for reflection. I strongly believe in a role for a literary audience—something not simply as a passive recipient of information but as an active respondent to questions, suggestions, and lines of argument—enticements (to use a more seductive word).

To give my own miniature essays their boundaries and focus, I offer pieces coalescing around two of the art forms that have dominated most of my life: Theatre and Poetry. Theatre first came to me through my mother, who entertained her three children (I was the eldest) with sock puppet plays and readings from children's stories. Theatre remained in my life all through high school and university, as I produced, directed, sometimes designed, and acted in one-act plays, scenes from plays, and full-length productions.

I did a M.A. thesis on *Hamlet*, although in this case the emphasis was on academic explication rather than theatre. Shakespeare was my literary and theatre idol, and he has remained so. As a teacher, I ran a drama club, and produced, directed, and/or acted in scenes from Shakespeare and plays by Edward Albee, T.S. Eliot, Eugene Ionesco, and Henri Ghéon.

When I began my freelance career as theatre reviewer and scholar in 1976, my exploration of theatre deepened and widened. It was not long before I began to write books on theatre—production histories, collections of theatre writing, and biography. I am a collector of great performances, besides being a collector of theatre books, and my enthusiasm in this regard is undiminished.

The little essays in the Theatre section of this book speak to some of my curiosities and obsessions: acting technique and acting issues (such as the private self and the role; the stage as a public forum; community theatre; pioneers and geniuses; the role of imagination; the role of feet; theatre as a responsibility; *et cetera*). This section invokes famous acting icons, such as Laurence Olivier, William Hutt, Heath Lamberts, and Vanessa Redgrave; it makes gestures of homage to the likes of Tennessee Williams, Ibsen, and Chekhov; it also invokes great acting teachers and actor-writers, such as Sanford Meisner, Stella Adler, Tadashi Suzuki, Simon Callow, and Oliver Ford Davies. I mix vignettes and anecdotes; impressionistic perspectives on Vivien Leigh and Cherry Jones, for instance; historical subjects (Boy Players, memorable first nights); tributes; and slices of autobiography. Some of my miniature essays are clearly meant to be provocative—never for the sake of mere provocation, however. All are meant to be lures for meditation or further contemplation, and I make no apology for their cosmopolitanism.

The Poetry section is also saturated with personal interests and obsessions. It, too, is sometimes anecdotal, without cancelling meditation. A reader can get a sense of some of the challenges of poetry readings (for both the poet and audience), questions of form, and some of the craft that creates poetry, as well as some of the mundane challenges to poets. The miniature essays are sometimes satirical, sometimes didactic—but never in an academic manner. This section makes reference to poetry from Armenia, Japan, Iran, England, Canada, and the U.S. The breadth of its cosmopolitanism is not intended to be merely exotic but to take a small measure of poetry's internationalism. It doesn't avoid some of the darkness or bleakness of contemporary poetry, and it provides insights into my personal sensibility.

Taken together, the pieces give a sampling of why I am drawn to Theatre and Poetry. Much of both genres can be disappointing at times. Theatre is built on illusion, of course, and Poetry comes out of dreaming by way of imagining, reflecting, and re-making. They are not useful the way car mechanics or accounting can be, but they are indispensable to me because both are important parts of my life. And my writing on them is also an important part of my life. But these pieces are not the last words on anything. Take them as opening gambits, pieces of larger bits to be hammered out of life and art, or simply opening sentences rather than finishing ones.

As I look back on the two themes of Theatre and Poetry, I realize how they have sometimes overlapped in my life. I think of poetry as performance and not simply as words on a page. Just as the best Theatre does not simply tell a story or amuse or appeal to our feelings, but compels us to reflect, and to understand the darker and deeper significances of characters and events, so Poetry also has ground in common with Theatre. In fact, many poets (such as the late Earle Birney, Ted Hughes, Anne Carson, and Margaret Atwood) have written plays, and many poets have been very theatrical in spoken performance. Both genres recognize potentiality and actuality. Consequently, both have an existential value. The vignettes and reflections are meant to attract the reader's interest to certain people in certain places and in certain times. While some of the matter is deliberately light, some more profound, the essays are essentially a breezy conversation with myself and interested readers.

Theatre

PART ONE

ON ACTING

Keith Garebian as 2nd Tempter in The Genesian Players
production of *Murder in the Cathedral* by T.S. Eliot,
directed by Rudy Stoeckel, St. Patrick's Church,
Montreal, February 1978.

Completing the Sentence, Completing the Thought

WILLIAM HUTT EXPLAINED TO ME THAT, IN HIS ACTING, HE always preferred to leave a thought unfinished. He said it was like singing "Come to me, my melancholy ..." and not uttering the final word "baby," allowing the audience to complete the sentence. I have thought about the implications ever since.

When we're part of an audience at a play, we're obviously willing to forego solitude, interrupt or suspend private reverie and internal monologue, and to submit, instead, to a communal, sometimes crowded experience. We're not allowed to finish our own mental sentences because the playwright's text is a complete thing, and actors prefer to utter the sentences as decreed—unless there is great acting on stage, where the actor uses a subtle, expert technique that coaxes, entices, incites, or provokes a spectator to complete his thought process while completing or, perhaps, half completing an action.

Only the very great actors or actresses—Laurence Olivier, Michael and Vanessa Redgrave, Maggie Smith, Judi Dench, Albert Finney, Cherry Jones, Daniel Day Lewis, Marlon Brando, Christopher Plummer, or William Hutt, for example—could show theatre intruding on life, stealing bits from it, transforming these pieces, yet delivering a tantalizing invitation to the most alert, most sensitive in the audience to fill in some of the gaps created by the mystery of character and thought.

But if we say that great acting leaves a little unsaid and that gap can be filled by a spectator, does this mean that there is something predictable even in great acting, for how would the spectator know what to fill in unless it could be eloquently anticipated? On the other hand, by filling in what is left unsaid, the spectator is not a mere voyeur but an active mental or spiritual participant by being complicit in the very process of creation.

No great acting is ever definable, and no great acting can ever have completeness. But can great acting exist without a great audience that is creatively complicit in the mimesis?

The Private Self
and the Role

WILLIAM HUTT WAS ADAMANT IN HIS CLAIM THAT AN ACTOR could never *become* another person on stage. He argued that acting was always a process of using one's own identity in disguise as another without losing the essence of that personal identity. In other words, a Hutt Lear was always the Lear in Hutt, just as an Olivier Hamlet could be only the Hamlet in Olivier. This idea has been reformulated by other acting eminences, one of whom is Simon Callow, who has written of the overlapping between character and actor: "Another person is coursing through your veins, is breathing through your lungs. But of course, it's not. It's only you— another arrangement of you." To which Oliver Ford Davies adds that an actor can only play aspects of oneself, not some construct of another person.

A penetrating wisdom because no matter how skilful the makeup and costuming, how accurate the accent, how practised the performance, the seasoned spectator always finds the actor in the role—even on film where disguise has been taken to extraordinary heights. It might take five minutes or thirty, but eventually one sees Alec Guinness behind the hooked nose and oily locks of his Fagin or Marlon Brando behind the puffy cheeks, sunken eyes, and tired stoop of his Don Corleone or Meryl Streep in any of her versatile imitations.

The private self, buried by disguise, comes to light because of its authenticity. And no amount of acquired mannerism or rehearsed style could ever mask that private self. The question is just how much or how deep or what texture that private self has.

Olivier, the supreme actor of my time, had an unparalleled amount of characters (on stage, screen, and television) within his self. But he himself did not really know what that self was because it was like water that took on the shape of the vessel (the role) it filled. Joan Plowright (his third wife) confessed that she often did not know what role he would assume in daily life from day to day. Olivier himself admitted that even he did not know what his real self was, though there were roles on which he placed his enduring stamp (Archie Rice in *The Entertainer* and Edgar in *Dance of Death*) that he himself felt were pieces of the real Olivier.

The Art of Being Private in Public

ACTING IS THE ART OF BEING PRIVATE IN PUBLIC——AS WILLIAM Hutt believed. Of course, he meant a stage privacy, a dramatization or comic expression or tragicomic exploration of that interiority.

His credo implicitly accepted the fact that the stage is a public forum, where the interior of a room (the set) allows the internal thoughts and feelings of a character to be externalized.

Naturally, it is through language or the word itself that the externalization proceeds. As Shakespeare well recognized in his use of soliloquies. And soliloquies should always be taken as truthful because the character alone on stage cannot be openly lying to himself when disclosing his innermost thoughts and feelings. He has no discernible reason to hide his private self—unless he were suffering from a pathology that the playwright fails to reveal.

As Oliver Ford Davies puts it: "When it's clear that the audience are being addressed, then it's a form of public, even political, act." But Shakespeare was careful not to overuse the soliloquy.

Watching Your Father
Die on Stage

Many years ago, when I was still active in community theatre in Montreal, my son Michael (who was only about five or six at the time) was brought by his mother to a performance of Albee's *The Zoo Story*, in which I was playing Jerry, the greatly disturbed, alienated being with a long cry of discontent. I had been taking him to live theatre ever since he was four, and he was a very alert spectator, deeply drawn to a story and its characters. I used to read to him every night, and he loved listening, especially to stories from the Bible—the ones that were filled with dramatic incident, such as the tale of King David and his rebellious son Absalom who led a revolt against his father and was killed during the battle in a wood. The upshot of the tale was the circumstance of his death: Absalom's long hair became entangled in the branches of an oak tree as the mule he was riding ran beneath it. One of his inveterate enemies, Joab, the King's commander, slew him with three arrows to the heart. When King David heard the news, he was overcome with agonizing grief and let out a howl: "O my son, Absalom, my son, my son Absalom! Would God had I died for thee, O Absalom, my son, my son!"

Born with theatre in my blood, I would do the howl with as much genuine emotion as I could muster, and my son was visibly moved and disturbed. Whether he felt sad for Absalom or sadder for heartbroken David I am not sure, but he certainly identified with my outcry, and begged: "O, Daddy, stop!"

Yet, as much as this tale shook him to the core, he would beg me to re-read it to him often.

Not long after, he would listen to me learning lines from *The Zoo Story*. In fact, when my fellow-actor, the one playing Peter (Jerry's foil, a complacent, publishing executive, married with two daughters, cats, and parakeets) rehearsed with me in my suburban living-room, my son was all eyes and ears. Soon after my fellow-actor had left, Michael was able to repeat huge chunks of the dialogue—not just mine, but Peter's as well. So incredulous was I that a tyke could listen so attentively and memorize very adult dialogue so quickly that I pulled out a tape-recorder and recorded his mimicry. He had the words down pat, along with the intonations. And while it was highly amusing to hear him enacting both roles, it was highly precocious, not to mention slightly weird, as well:

JERRY: But you wanted boys.
PETER: Well ... naturally, every man wants a son, but ...
JERRY: (Lightly mocking) But that's the way the cookie
    crumbles?

And then my son came to the show. He was seeing me on stage for the very first time and, while he was silent during Peter's frightened and frightful animal rages, I heard him sniffle during the "fight" scene on the bench when Jerry goads Peter into battling for ownership or space on that bench, culminating in a violent stabbing when Jerry deliberately engineers his own death. Then, at the sight of his father with a switchblade and stage blood on his hands, and in the throes of death, my son could not stop himself. His sniffle became a sob, and the sobbing continued unabated. Though my stage concentration was strong, I could not but hear those little boy's sobs.

Jump forward many years to the death of my sister Elma from cancer at the age of thirty-six, and the sight and sounds of my parents grieving at her casket before it was sealed for her burial. Michael watched as his grandparents, weighed down by grief, let out sounds that he had never heard before anywhere. My mother's were a low sobbing hum, a keening; my father's was louder—an awful sound of a parent's untimely, unnatural loss. The sound of age bemoaning an all-too-early death of a child who had been his undeclared but definite favourite of his three offspring. An animal sound that I had never heard before, not even when my father recounted the awful brutalities of his Armenian history and his people's genocide at the hands of the Turks. Not even the deep melancholy at memories of his mother's sudden death by heartbreak and hunger. That had been awful enough; this death was worse. She had been named after his beloved mother whom he had lost when he was but five.

And yet my son had not wept this time. He was shaken, all right, but he remained silent.

There are, after all, many ways of dying. Just as there are many ways of grieving.

Does dying as a stage actor in a role prepare one for real death?

Shakespeare probably believed so. It is not surprising that he's one of the most quoted poets at funerals and memorial services. As Domenic Dromgoole puts it in his beautifully written, wise essays in *Will & Me*: "The theme of 'Fear no more ...,' 'Full fathom five ...' and 'Like as the waves ...' is pretty unequivocal. You live and then you die. And though you may turn into something rich and strange, what is certain is that the scythe will mow, and you will turn to dust. What mention there is of heaven is pretty muted compared to the toughness of all the finality." (165) Shakespeare did not seek to beautify death, even in romantic tragedy (*Romeo and Juliet*). He does offer very human, very loving benedictions for loved ones in plays and sonnets, but the point of his stories is: "To accept the end of the story with the same excitement as the beginning and the same delirious pleasure as the middle was, if anything, what Shakespeare was trying to help us towards." And his stage actors and actresses incarnate his deepest beliefs about death and grief—all linked to his own life.

Community Theatre and
Why One Goes into Acting

Most stage performers, unless they attend theatre school, start with community theatre. In fact, the relatively short history of professional Canadian theatre begins with little regional and community theatres, with amateur groups in Montreal, Ottawa, and Toronto leading the way. Some of the very best professional English-speaking actors in Montreal (Len Watt, Walter Massey, Victor Knight, Norma Springford, Ann Wickham) had their start as part of such community theatres, and one of the leading producers in that city also formed a company that mixed amateur and professional actors. That was Mary Morter, the founder of Instant Theatre in 1965, a lunch time group that included actors who were well known to local television and radio audiences. I was among the performers in one of her groups. Well, perhaps it was more of an *ad hoc* group, but it included professionals George Carron and Don Scanlon. I acted opposite Carron in a one-act piece (*Coffee House*), directed by Scanlon. I was also part of an evening in a Westmount church, when colleagues and I enacted scenes from plays. Morter invited Mavor Moore to adjudicate (kindly). One of the excerpts was from *The Corn is Green*, and I remember him remarking of the general fare: "The corn is green, indeed!" His ambiguity was diplomatically skilful and utterly consistent with his reputation as a cultural politician and ambassador for the arts.

I did not know much about Mary Morter's impressive background at the time, but I remain grateful to her for what she accomplished with her generous heart in Montreal. I have since learned that she kept English-language theatre alive and healthy in lean times before it received national subsidies. Born Lilian Mary Jones in Gloucester to a Welsh carpet factory owner, Mary never went to acting school but was always involved with the arts. She received most of her training with the Cheltenham Players in Gloucestershire, and in 1951 she married Eric Morter, an engineer, before immigrating to Canada in 1957. She founded her first amateur group, The Questers, First Place winner in the Dominion Drama Festival in 1962, and after she moved to Montreal, she launched Instant Theatre in a 99-seat venue at Place Ville Marie. However, she did not list herself as Artistic Director. That honour went to Sean Mulcahy, an Irish-born actor she had known from Cheltenham. Instant Theatre led to the founding of Centaur Theatre, and the country's introduction to Maurice Podbrey of South Africa, who became its long time Artistic Director, and with whom I (as a freelance theatre critic) had numerous rhetorical exchanges offstage, some of which highlighted the common but unnecessarily adversarial nature of the actor/critic dynamic.

What I also learned from an obituary after Mary Morter's passing at the age of 84 in 2008 was that the name Instant Theatre came into being because she had negotiated financial support from an instant food company that suddenly withdrew from the enterprise, leaving her little option but to sell sandwiches to the audience. The frequent rustling of sandwich wrappings proved irritating to the actors, but the shows went on.

I also joined other community amateur groups, having already proved my acting chops at university (where Ann Wickham was impressed enough by my acting in *The Zoo Story* to recommend that I audition at La Poudrière) and then becoming First Player in the first English language version of Henri Ghéon's *Passion Play*, performed outdoors at St. Joseph's Oratory in Montreal, under the direction of Valerie Bowyer. There exists in an official Oratory calendar a full-colour shot of me making a very dramatic gesture at one of the Stations of the Cross. Much later, I would be part of another group that staged Eliot's *Murder in the Cathedral* in St. Patrick's Basilica. The setting was magnificent in one way, and absolutely appropriate for the murder of the saint. However, acoustics were dreadful, and when I began as Tempter (I also would play one of the Murderers), I was chagrined to learn that my fellow thespians and I were audible only as a dreadful rumble. There went Eliot's glorious text. There went our acting pride.

The whole business of amateur and semi-amateur theatre companies raises questions about artistic standards and the distinctions between amateur and professional. Sometimes the boundaries blur, and it is a fallacy to think that only professional actors can have a sustained technique. And why is it that professionals (even at the Stratford Festival) can seldom pass muster when pretending to be clumsy amateurs as in the Pyramus and Thisbe sections of *A Midsummer Night's Dream*? They tend to be dreadfully condescending and overact outrageously, embarrassing themselves in the process. In pretending to be hams, they become utterly hammy. It's rather like parodying a parody.

More intriguing than any such discussion is the motivation for acting. Why does one go into acting in the first place? Is it because we wish to have fluid identities, to dream ourselves into whatever world or skin we wish? Is it to leave our humdrum world behind and escape to a world of illusion in the full knowledge that we eventually have to return to the mundane one?

Is it to participate in a communal sharing that will make us feel joined to fellow beings? Is it (as some of our more pompous professionals claim) to discover truths about ourselves by exploring other identities? Or is it something even more basic, more particularly human—a need to be noticed?

In a television interview by James Lipton for an *Inside the Actors Studio* episode, Dustin Hoffman related an experience with the late Laurence Olivier, with whom he had worked on *Marathon Man*. When Hoffman asked Olivier: "We all wonder what it is that makes us do what we do. Do you have an answer? Tell me, what's the reason we do what we do?" Olivier, who was steadily on painkillers for his several ailments, dragged himself up on his painful feet, and leaned over at almost face level with Hoffman: "You want to know why, dear boy? Look at me, look at me, look at me, look at me, look at me, look at me, look at me!" It was rapid, and it was nakedly candid, without any concession to camouflage.

Perhaps the radical motivation is our need to be noticed—to be made significant in however small a way that can be mustered. Being noticed means that you are not ignored. Being noticed means that you can have something to say, something to show—perhaps a strong passion or a far from trivial thought. Attention, however short, is being paid to you.

You are not being brushed aside.

There is a fundamental existential desire, perhaps what could be called a metaphysical one because I am not equating such a need to be noticed with, say, a narcissist's or a media whore's need to dominate a news cycle.

Ego is always a part of any actor, indeed of any human being. Ego is good if you know how to use it and how to locate it as part of a healthy self.

Child's Play

Acting (in the sense of pretending) comes naturally to children who love to play at Cowboys and Indians (to use politically incorrect language), and impersonate astronauts, cops, robbers, animals, birds, or whatever. Perhaps, imitation in such play-acting or pretending is a rehearsal for the adult world, that itself often requires grown-ups to pretend to feel things that they don't really feel. Perhaps, such play is a game of Control and Conversion: a child's wish to manage a situation, create a parallel world, create a sense of safety, indulge a fantasy, *et cetera*.

At 70, William Hutt impersonated a five-year-old boy at a birthday party with charmingly mischievous credibility in A.R. Gurney's *The Dining Room*, even as he sported a silver head, Van Dyke beard, party hat, bowtie, and circular horn-rimmed glasses. Hutt's Brewster had a twinkle, a gleam that actress Patricia Collins, who was portraying a five-year-old girl opposite him, found impossible to describe. Hutt's impersonation displayed his superb power of observation, and this made him seem ageless.

Actors pretend all the time. In fact, many of them do not allow their inner child to go underground—which is all to the good when they are playing roles on stage, but unfortunate when they allow childish intemperance and ego to get the better of their judgment offstage.

Children can manage demons when they are play-acting, but real-life demons are much harder to control and conquer in adult life.

Which brings to mind Oscar Wilde's witty epigram: "One's Real Life is the Life One Does Not Lead."

Do Actors Love the Audience?

LAURENCE OLIVIER'S EXPRESS INTENT WAS TO SEDUCE AN audience—not simply the women but the men as well. When he performed on stage, audiences lined up overnight to see him perform. They would besiege him for autographs (there were no selfies in those days) and he would usually comply, unless his schedule disallowed this.

But one of his reputed backstage rituals was to get into costume and makeup, walk briefly on stage before the curtain, and curse the audience—opening night critics, especially—in an undertone. But, then, who isn't a critic at a play, especially these days, when even the most fatuous opinions are aired with the bloviating narcissistic ignorance of a Donald Trump?

Was Olivier actually contemptuous or was he merely practising a form of self-therapy and self-immunization? After all, the performing arts are the only genres where there is immediate reaction. Writers may have to wait a year or two to receive critical reaction in print, but actors know in the instant if they are being loved or detested. This must be wounding in the extreme, and, perhaps, extreme suffering demands extreme measures of self-protection, even if Olivier's example proves to be an illusion or delusion of self-defence.

Yet even audiences need to be loved, especially by those they applaud or revere. Is there anything worse than an actor or actress acting like a diva after a show and rushing off to a taxi or limousine while fans stand patiently at the stage door, awaiting a few seconds of their time, some sweet acknowledgment of the huge money that has been shelled out for just a couple of hours of entertainment? Recently, I joined fans after a thrilling performance of *The Color Purple* outside the Jacobs Theatre in New York. I was also lining up for autographs because as a theatre critic, I, too, am a fan of great performers, and there was at least one, undeniably great performance in the musical—that of Cynthia Erivo, a British import, and a powerhouse talent compressed into her short, muscular physique. Ms. Erivo was the last to emerge from the stage door, and she proved to be generous with her time. But before her appearance, there was Heather Headley's. She had played Shug Avery, the sexually provocative blues singer. Ms. Headley dutifully made her way from one side of the cordon to the other, posing for selfies, signing glossy photos and programs. Someone thanked her for taking so much time with fans, and Ms. Headley smiled in return and said: "You are the ones who paid big money and have been waiting patiently outside. It's the least I could do."

That's what I call class.

That's deserving of fan love because it returns love for love.

On Style in a Play

STYLE IN A PLAY IS NOT REALLY ABOUT WEARING A COSTUME well or wielding a fan with aplomb; it is not really about how the actor stands or sits, or how he pronounces certain words and phrases. Style may well be a case of knowing what play you're in. If you're doing a period piece—well, let me rephrase this because every play is actually a piece in its own specific period. If you're doing an 18th century play, you cannot act as if you're in a 21st century play—unless the original play has been adapted and moved out of its original context. Or if you're performing Tennessee Williams, you should not move or sound as if you were doing Noel Coward.

Some playwrights, such as Coward or Wilde or Sheridan, cannot be moved out of their periods without diminishing or completely ruining the plays. Others (even Shaw and especially Shakespeare) can, if you have a sharp director and an accomplished cast.

Sounds obvious enough, yet many performers have immense trouble talking about style. Perhaps they should move beyond setting (time and place) to the language itself of a piece because, if the text is well written, it will summon up its own style—unless the director imposes his own concept or context on the production. Virginia Woolf once wrote: "Style is a very simple matter; it is all rhythm."

However, I don't agree that style is all that simple because rhythm can be a tricky thing, depending on the quality or genius of the playwright. The style of language in Arthur Miller's *The Crucible* is quite different from that in his *Death of a Salesman*, and it is easy enough to perceive this clearly. But how about Shakespeare, who is adept at many different rhythms in the same play? As in *Hamlet*, the Henry plays, *As You Like It*, *Love's Labour's Lost*, *et cetera*. Perhaps in cases such as Shakespeare's rich plays, a sound instinct for textures of language and rhythm is a requisite, assisted by acting technique.

The Lure of Technique

CREATIVE PEOPLE MAKE A HABIT OF STUDYING TECHNIQUE. In fact, a writer who doesn't concern himself with another writer's technique will probably not improve or extend his or her own. Similarly, in the theatre, an actor who neglects technique neglects an essential part of acting.

But technique can be a trap, depending on how it is practised. Laurence Olivier was universally celebrated for his acting technique, yet his versatility and virtuosity were considered to be impediments to his ability to reach the emotional truth of a role. It was generally held that he was an external actor—as opposed to the actor who subordinates technique to emotional truth. It was said that he could *act* pain rather than show it truthfully, that he could *act* tragedy rather than be a tragedian.

However, there is another perspective. Olivier's technique was so wide, so masterly that it lured an audience into its web so that other aspects of his acting were diminished. His acting had the most versatile tropes of rhythm, pacing, and mood. His movement was fluent, and athletic at times. When he played a soldier, an audience never doubted the veracity of his performance. When he played a romantic hero, he could seduce both genders of his audience. When he played Othello all out as black, even black actors applauded his amazing *chutzpah* and versatility. And his range on stage and screen was remarkable: everything from Shakespeare, Sophocles, Sheridan, Goldsmith, Osborne, Shaw, Congreve, Ibsen, Anouilh, Chekhov, Pinter, Feydeau, Farquhar, Wilder, O'Neill, and Strindberg to Ionesco, Williams, Inge, Behrman, Fry, John Ford, Rattigan, Maugham, Greene, Trevor Griffiths, John Mortimer, and R.C. Sherriff. Not all were triumphant, but none was less than interesting.

Peter Ustinov once remarked that Olivier could act roles better than most people could live them. And why was this so? Because Olivier, with immense scepticism about the idea of genius, believed that he first had a duty to learn, expand, and consolidate his craft—which is to say the technique with which to perfect his acting instruments of voice, face, body, and imagination. Moreover, he was never shy about daring to look or sound absurd in rehearsals; nor was he reticent about sexual ambivalence. He could be camp; he could be tender. He could be boldly masculine; he could be subtly feminine. When he played foppish Tattle, he could walk backward feverishly across the top of a stone wall while entertaining lewd thoughts of what lay below Miss Prue's girdle. When he was Coriolanus, he could be proud, nervously embarrassed, and teasingly ambiguous about being dominated by his mother. And his Othello gleamed with a wide black chest, strode gracefully on bare feet, was frankly carnal but also exhibited a sexual flirtatiousness.

His technique was never so perfect, so cold as to stifle real passion. He always dealt in physical, observed realities—not in abstract nouns or adjectives. It was just that his technique was so dazzling that acting aficionados could not help but study it rather than experience it as part of the machinery and fuel of a role.

So, when I keep hearing from his critics (often younger actors who have the convictions of their mediocrity) that they could see the wheels spinning, that he was oh, so calculated, or that he was clever without being moving, I retort: "Yes, Olivier wanted to perpetuate the *glamour* of acting. He wanted his audiences to gasp in awe but he was never just self-concerned. He wanted to exhibit his physical, vocal, and emotional range as a lure to fellow actors and audiences. He wanted to be the culmination of a race of super-actors."

In these ways, he was the most generous of actors because he was a *giving* actor—that is giving of himself, giving of his immense talent and skill, giving so much of his vocation that his talent eventually cannibalized him. Near the end of his career, his marvellous voice had dwindled, his physique (burdened by numerous ailments) withered, and he was almost spent.

The one thing that still flamed from time to time was his will to find a way of giving yet more. And he did in his Lear for television when his technique was no longer as supple or versatile. Instead the purer actor filled the role in the final act—an old man, a king who had given away his kingdom all for naught, a father who had hurt the one daughter who truly loved him, a king who learned his final wisdom too late. Here was a great actor who had seemingly made the act of being simple and honest the culmination of an astonishingly virtuosic career.

It was as if Olivier had removed a theatre mask to find a true face.

He had become a naked actor.

Researching the Role

WHEN SERVING AS A PANELLIST FOR A SYMPOSIUM ON WILLIAM Hutt's Inuit Lear, I heard the moderator—a professional actor and acting teacher—claim that it would be very helpful for the actor playing Othello to visit a black community and interact with its members in order to experience what it could mean to be a black person in a predominantly white society. His assertion was thunder in my ears, but of the wrong sort. It was tantamount to suggesting that an actor playing Greek tragedy should speak to a contemporary Greek person in order to reach the essence of classical tragedy.

Whatever became of the actor's imagination? Is it possible to be a good actor, much less a great one, if one does not have a path to transformation by imagining the world of the character? Part of the problem of the modern actor—especially the English "cerebralists" and the American "Methodists"—is their relegation of acting to research, either of the academic or the self-absorbed type. According to the great mime teacher Jacques Lecoq, the most important muscle in the body is IMAGINATION.

Once again, it is wise to turn to Shakespeare who addressed the topic in *A Midsummer Night's Dream*:

The poet's eye, in a fine frenzy rolling,
Doth glance from heaven to earth, from earth to heaven,

And as imagination bodies forth
The form of things unknown, the poet's pen
Turns them to shapes, and gives to airy nothing
A local habitation and a name.

Oliver Ford Davies cites director Declan Donnellan's thoughts on the same subject: "In the beginning was not the word. In the beginning was the imagination, which longs to communicate with others. Words are one means of doing this. But no word is ever properly understood unless it has been spontaneously created by the imagination."

Great Roles
Can Be Cannibalistic

Laurence Olivier believed great Shakespearean roles could be cannibalistic. He was preparing his stage Othello at the time, and anyone familiar with his hours of careful makeup and months of gym work would understand, perhaps, what he meant. Always one who built a character from the outside in, Olivier worked on transforming his natural speaking voice (a baritone tending towards tenor notes in passages of high-flown rhythm) so that he could have something suggestive of the Moor's velvet black voice. He also adopted a rather alien accent—something faintly Caribbean at times—with a strong sense of rhythm that made his spoken delivery sound almost exotic—the very justification for thinking him an outsider in Venice. His vowel sounds deepened, his consonants thickened, and he could sound guttural as well as high strung.

He would fastidiously apply hours of Max Factor 2880 to his body, then a lighter brown, then Negro Number 2, a stronger brown. "Brown on black to give a rich mahogany. Then the great trick: that glorious half yard of chiffon with which I polished myself all over until I shone." And he did, gleaming a smooth ebony. The eyebrows and lashes were thickened with mascara, the lips coloured carmine, and Olivier made it a point of learning how to stride like a magnificently self-assured black man with his own particular, muscular rhythm. His many hours of gym work expanded his biceps and chest, adding to a sense of might and size. Maggie Smith related how he could swiftly lift her off the floor with a single arm. Other fellow-actors attested that, at the top of his passionate outbursts (and Othello has one powerful rant after another), Olivier's neck would swell to twice its normal size.

His was clearly and vividly an Othello who had never suffered from thin skin. Olivier's Moor was the very incarnation of Negritude from nappy hair and bare chest and feet to his animal stride and sexual confidence. In the only book he ever (co)wrote on acting—rather tritely entitled *On Acting*, Olivier described how he developed his walk for the role: "I should walk like a soft black leopard. Sensuous. He should grow from the earth, the rich brown earth, warmed by the sun." His would be a bare-footed, lithe, dignified, sensual Moor, whose impulses and emotions were always close to the surface, ready to erupt like volcanic lava. The actor's technical equipment would help him keep the lid on the role when necessary but, when the explosions happened, their power was overwhelming.

After the performance, Olivier would remove his make-up slowly, and after a long soak in a bathtub, he would emerge (we have the reliable testimony of Joan Plowright, Lady Olivier) as pink as a shrivelled shrimp.

Was this the role—with its virtually superhuman demands on his acting equipment—that accelerated his physical decline? Were its emotional demands too much even for the modern theatre's greatest actor to bear in addition to his excessive workload as Artistic Director of Britain's Royal National Theatre? If not by itself, then surely as an aggregate in combination with his other great roles, such as Archie Rice, James Tyrone, and Captain Edgar.

Olivier could certainly have offered his second wife as further evidence of how a great role can cannibalize a performer: Vivien Leigh's Blanche du Bois.

What Vivien Leigh found important in Blanche was a beauty of spirit, imagination, and mind, a fragile beauty that shrank from harsh memories, including of her own abnormal sexual desire. Blanche carries a secret within herself: her brief, tragic marriage to a homosexual who killed himself. Leigh was a nymphomaniac during her eerily abnormal psychic attacks, when she would prowl around the seedier parts of London, seeking men.

Yet, Leigh, like Blanche, needed great kindness, great tenderness to survive. The key to her interpretation was Stella's line: "Nobody, nobody, was tender and trusting as she was."

Tender and trusting. A pale butterfly shrinking from harsh light, trapped within a suffocating room steaming with Stanley's animal urges and brutality. A butterfly in panic because of an anticipated hammer stroke by this lusty killer.

Leigh slept little as she prepared for the film version, opposite Brando. Blanche stayed on her mind so totally that there were times when she fully believed she was the character—cynical, hard, mad.

And Vivien Leigh was manic depressive in real life, a nymphomaniac at times, an actress who took shock therapy treatment, and who, at moments of real-life hysteria, would scream out Blanche's terror-stricken "Fire!"

For Vivien Leigh, Blanche du Bois was a case of the mask's fusing with the real face, of the actor's ritual mask's exposing Leigh's soul-shuddering cry of anguish.

The mask took over, destroying physically and psychologically the sublime actress in the process.

Boy Players

SHAKESPEARE'S GREAT FEMALE ROLES WERE ESSAYED BY BOY players. This must have been astonishing simply in terms of gender ambiguity, not to mention technical skill. Think, for example, of the boy playing Rosalind in *As You Like It*. The boy player has to first pretend to be a woman, and then the woman pretending to be a man, yet one who at the heart of disguise is a woman falling in love with another man. Sounds as complicated as it is to perform. And the boy player attempting Rosalind would have to have had real genius to pull off such a complicated impersonation that requires a matrix of wit, eroticism, virtuoso verse speaking, and modulations of tone. There are not many seasoned, well-trained actresses today who succeed in the role. So, was Shakespeare challenging the boy players and audiences of his day with a huge role involving gender ambiguity or was he revelling in the freedom such imposture provided him as a dramatist?

A related question I have is why boys can impersonate women far more convincingly than girls can impersonate men? As a pupil at an all-boys high school (run by Jesuits) in Bombay, I participated in many stage productions, many of which necessitated cross-gender representation. I recall one particular case where we performed scenes from *The Merchant of Venice*, and one of my peers, a Hindu boy with a remarkably sweet disposition though not necessarily a feminine face, impersonated Portia to good effect. We had no knowledge of the issue of colour-blind, gender-bending casting because many of us were multi-racial and of an entire range of skin colour. Our productions were always colour-blind and multi-racial. With the Shakespeare, the matter of gender impersonation was simply accepted as being congruent with the Elizabethan convention of boy players, and our Portia did not in the least offer a stereotypical performance. Instead, he moved gracefully but without overdoing the feminine movement, and he spoke clearly and credibly, especially Portia's famous "The quality of mercy" speech. I was not then a practising theatre critic, of course, but I could recognize a false, hammy performance when I saw one. When I was on stage with him, I did not think of his being a teenager impersonating a woman. I saw a Portia inside a teenage boy.

Many decades later, I had the opportunity to see the Grand Kabuki of Japan at the Lincoln Center in New York, and what fascinated me the most were the *onnagata*—the male actors who impersonated female characters. Without being condescending to women, these *onnagata* seemed to know the very inwardness of women. It wasn't a matter of costuming or makeup, or even necessarily their mincing steps; after a few moments of observing them on stage, I forgot they were actually young men who were playing female roles. What I saw were real women or, what was more fascinating, the very *spirit* of women in action.

But why is it that hardly any actresses succeed in male impersonation? The few who have—Vanessa Redgrave (*Second Serve*), Tilda Swinton (*Orlando*), Felicity Huffman (*Transamerica*), Hillary Swank (*Boys Don't Cry*), Glenn Close and Janet McTeer (*Albert Nobbs*)—were all in film or television roles, where the enhancements of editing, costuming, makeup, lighting, and other effects can easily enhance an illusion. However, this qualification aside, these actresses were spectacularly effective, especially when compared to the gender parodies or vulgarizations performed by scores of others, some of whom were, in fact, transgender performers. Is it because mere technique is inadequate to pull off the illusion? Is it because such impersonation requires a genius that can find the essence, the subtext, the inscape of the specific woman being represented?

Grammar of the Feet

JUST AS DANCE IS DEPENDENT ON FEET, AS IS TRADITIONAL Kabuki, stage acting reveals the importance of the actor's feet. And we know that realism requires an actor to master different ways of walking in accordance with different characters' deportments and movements. A Romeo would necessarily walk differently from a Falstaff, just as a Rosalind would move quite differently from a Mistress Quickly. A drunken walk has to look different from the movement of one in a bedroom farce. Therefore, the feet can often be as important as the voice in the creation of a stage character.

Heath Lamberts once complained to me that television directors often destroyed a farce performance by not showing the farcical actor's feet in motion as he dashed in and out of doors or came to huffing-and-puffing rest at a crucially important moment. Showing the feet would have captured a measure of the rhythm and tempo of the comic acting, and would also have distinguished one character from another.

Tadashi Suzuki explains that, in the traditional Japanese performing arts, "the equilibrium, the source of strength, emanates in all directions from the pelvic area, which radiates energy into horizontal space." Feet establish an intimate connection with the ground and thereby with a sense of equilibrium. And another practitioner outlined eleven sitting habits of the Japanese as techniques that actors could practise and master for the stage.

Given these fundamental facts, why do film and television directors continue to neglect feet in performances? Is there anything worse than shooting an actor in tight close-up when what is required is a medium long shot of how he actually moves? Ever see a filmed ballet ruined by a close-up of the dancer's face and chest rather than of his miraculous feet? Think how limited our pleasure would be if we could not see the feet of Fred Astaire, Ginger Rogers, Eleanor Powell, Gene Kelly, Cyd Charisse, Gwen Verdon, Chita Rivera, Margot Fonteyn, Rudolf Nureyev, Mikhail Baryshnikov, and other great dancers.

Think, too, of how outrageous it would be not being able to *see* Olivier's different walks as Heathcliff, Archie Rice, Othello, Crassus, or Creakle.

Great acting often demands great feet.

Size in *The Glass Menagerie*

WATCHING CHERRY JONES CREATE HER AMANDA WINGFIELD on Broadway in Tennessee Williams' memory play, I rediscovered a truth about great acting. All the earlier stage Amandas I had seen hardly reached beyond literal realism as they chattered about Southern cotillions, gentleman-callers, and table manners. They were girlish, fluttery, silly, amusing, vain, protective of Laura, angry at Tom, sometimes touching, and deluded. But none had dared enlarge the role the way Cherry Jones did in 2013. The actress used mime, almost danced with her hands, as she fumed and fretted, coaxed and recoiled, daring the audience to find her absurd while she expressed Amanda's desperate, fierce love. In other words, her acting choices were bold and rooted in a technique that did not shy away from magnifying the voice or body movement. She did not try to be a little, hard-pressed, nagging single mom or a mother dying a little internally every time she tried to shield her crippled daughter from life's various assaults. Cherry Jones treated Amanda as a character of dimension, and by adding to the role's stature, she also enlarged the pathos.

Great acting defies convention.

Great acting cannot be defined.

Great acting always makes a role seem minted for the first time.

And Tennessee Williams, because of his innate poetry of the spirit, wrote great roles for great actresses: for example, Vivien Leigh's Blanche, Anna Magnani's Serafina, Geraldine Page's Alexandra del Lago, Vanessa Redgrave's Lady Torrance, and Cherry Jones' Amanda Wingfield. Spellbinding, high risk, high definition performances that dared to reach deep down to the bruised souls of their characters without inhibition and yet with immense art and truth. An art that went far beyond craft into zones of sheer genius.

Taking Comedy Seriously

Over thirty years ago, two of the greatest Canadian comic actors were William Hutt and Heath Lamberts. Hutt was a master of the mechanics of "lying" in the theatre. He had the studied skill of seeming unstudied. I observed his performance as Sheridan Whiteside in *The Man who Came to Dinner* at the Grand Theatre, London, Ontario because it was a 20th century American farce, and it was not played at the Stratford Festival, where Hutt dominated productions from Shakespeare to Chekhov, Molière to Wilde.

The Kaufman-Hart comedy allowed him a central starring role, but it was largely a sedentary one, for Whiteside (the man who came unwillingly to dinner) sits in a wheelchair for most of the action after having slipped on ice outside and presumably broken a leg. Therefore, his roguishness and childishness have to be conveyed rhetorically and by physical effects chiefly from the neck up. The role can be played through the teeth, with biting consonants, and a crisp staccato of lordly orders to all and sundry. As the "world's rudest man," Hutt's acid comments as Whiteside came with icy composure, hitting his palate and clicking against his teeth.

Hutt could turn on a victim either through virtuoso consonance or by a brief but pointed bit of business, as when he lamented being "Tr—rr-app-edd!" Or when he reacted to his nurse's gentle admonition against his eating pecan butternut fudge by first pinning her with a merciless insult, and then licking his fudge-stained fingers. The Christmas dinner became a spectacle of him carving up the "turkeys" (his household and dinner guests) with irascible wit. But it was his gleaming teeth and wily smile that I shall always remember.

Heath Lamberts, of a much younger generation, had a chubby, puff-pastry face, a dumpling nose, and a doughy benignity on stage. His physiognomy seemed more suited to custard-pie comedy than to sophisticated farce or artful satire, and yet, he was magically plastic on stage. He could propel himself on small dainty feet, his eyes inflamed by some inner mischief, his mouth caught in its own pantomime, and his hands playing charades on themes of timorousness, anxiety, and narcissism.

As Monsieur Jourdain in Molière's *The Bourgeois Gentleman*, he was not simply a foolish tradesman deserving of a pratfall or public humiliation, but a human being with tight shoes, runs in his stockings, and a heart that was much bigger than his mind. He was the eternal child eternally seduced by fantasy, a fool bubbling with faults but also one who was endearingly vulnerable. He was the Jourdain for our time—the Jourdain in everyone who wants to be on par with his betters, the Jourdain who is bound to be found out as an overly romantic self-deluder, the masquerading child trapped in the awkward body of a pretentious social-climber. His Jourdain was in masquerade from the beginning, showing off awkwardly his rich Oriental robe with long red sleeves that sometimes entangled him.

The child in Jourdain was apparent in the carefree legs, swinging feet, and eager surveys of his attendants and visitors for their approval. He tried so hard to imitate his dancing master's reclining posture, producing comic absurdity from excruciating geometry. Pauses were interludes for a busy fidgeting. He chatted, flirted, applauded the dancers too early, and then tried to resist boredom by pushing back a drooping eyebrow with one plump finger. After he had slid farther and farther down his ornate chair, and fallen to the floor, part of him managed to disappear under the chair from where his snores were amplified.

Plasticity is often what defines physical clowning, and it is one of the many things that Lamberts had in abundance. When he essayed a minuet, he went up on his toes, but his heels and elbows were so out of joint that he seemed to be a moving compendium of disparate limbs. He skittered, slid, tripped, and lurched, but kept enjoying the attempt and energy of his own dancing. In his fencing lesson, his heels locked together and his torso bent perilously off centre, putting his entire body at risk of collapse. Unable to take his stance without using his foil as a lever to move his feet absurdly far apart, he lunged in overdrive and almost split himself from crotch to hip. Plasticity extended even to his voice. He stretched his mouth, pulling on his lips, and the breath came as a whine or gasp. His lesson in vowels and consonants degenerated into atonal dissonance.

Lamberts and Hutt both had the ability and facility to run off with a play, but both were expert at impersonation. Neither man could ever miss a trick, but their magic was not merely a question of tricks, but of something profoundly discovered and exposed. Both geniuses took their comedy seriously, creating eruptions of comic effervescence. The more serious they seemed to be about absurdity, the funnier they were.

Genius in Acting

A COMMON COMPLAINT FROM THEATRE SCHOLARS IS THAT theatre biographies often fail to define great acting. But this criticism is invalid because great acting—just like great music, great painting, or even great poetry—cannot be defined. Any artistic greatness defies categories, and definition needs categories. Such greatness cannot be pinned down like a butterfly on felt in a museum display. And when it comes to theatre acting, how does any critic do better than describe it in the most graphic, colourful sense that can never amount to anything more than a pale shadow of what actually transpired in performance? Moreover, in the case of a great performance, that performance is all but certain to change from night to night. This is not a law but empiric experience. That is why a great performer can swing from greatness to awfulness and back again in the same role in the same production.

I have seen it happen at Stratford with the late, great Kate Reid in Michel Tremblay's *Les Belles Soeurs*. I saw the production twice—the first time early in the run, and the second later. In the first instance, Reid seemed totally incongruous to the production and play. Worse, she seemed incompetent—uncertain of her choreography, shaky in voice, almost dazed by what was transpiring around her.

She looked like an actress who should have been forced into retirement, because all the gossip about her heavy drinking and smoking appeared to be true. Their physical toll was immense, and now, with seriously failing eyesight, Reid was giving credence to the fear that she was washed up. But then came my second trip to the same show, and I could hardly believe my eyes or ears. Kate Reid was in an entirely different acting zone, free of artificial mannerisms, her voice sturdy, her movements controlled. She made most of the others in the cast look mediocre—and they weren't.

I have heard others speak in shocked tones about other great actors—Olivier and Hutt, included—whose performances also swung from awful to great during a run. But shouldn't we allow for inconsistency in great acting? True greatness does not respect repetition. In fact, the two ideas are incompatible. It is impossible to guess how a great actor or actress will ever perform from performance to performance.

Take the case of Vanessa Redgrave. Trevor Nunn once advised Sheridan Morley who was to direct her in *Song at Twilight*: "Don't even try directing her. Clear a flight path where she can land on stage, look after the others, and just don't expect her ever to do the same thing two nights running because she won't, and you can save your breath about giving her notes—whatever she does tonight, she's not going to do tomorrow night."

The thrilling thing about such greatness is the suspense it builds for the spectator who simply cannot anticipate what the performer is going to do from moment to moment. Expect the unexpected because great acting is not about replication. It is about freedom and the essence of live theatre.

Great acting is mutable.

Even the greatest theatre critics—Bernard Shaw, Kenneth Tynan, Walter Kerr, John Lahr, and others—can never capture the essence of great acting. All they can do is impart a sense of how it felt to witness a great performance. Some of these critics are to be treasured for the palpable colour, flair, and vividness of their descriptions, but whatever they memorialize in words remains words, however great their writing performances.

Great acting melts away like a block of ice left out on a summer day.

Genius Can Sometimes Be Too Good for a Country

CℓⓄ

COMIC GENIUS IN THE THEATRE CAN SOMETIMES PROVE TOO good, too big for a country to handle with equanimity—especially a country proud of its puritanical work ethic and values that exist primarily as colonial nostalgia.

Is it because the genius is feared for its ability to beat the last breath of life out of propriety, modesty, and proportion?

Is it because of the country's taboo against cheerfulness, or, more pointedly, the chaos of crazy, inspired farce?

Is it because genius is feared for being strong personal expression pitted against the conventional balance of an ensemble?

Is it because genius has its own hunger that sucks up a company's energy, leaving mediocrity or the average exposed nakedly?

Is it because a country, brought up to be good-mannered and polite, cannot abide anything that appears to be rudely ridiculous, tragicomic, a travesty, a caricature, the special power of the clown beyond what we normally see in a circus or stand-up comedy or a drawing-room farce?

These questions are generated by my musing about the late Heath Lamberts, a comic genius who ruffled many feathers of directors and fellow-actors because of his comic anarchy.

Lamberts was born to be a clown. He renamed himself by disappearing into a trunk and re-emerging self-chris-tened. James Langcaster remade into Heath Lamberts. Bored at school, he yearned to act. His school gave up on him be-cause it did not know (like most schools) how to cope with his singular genius, and it sent him off rudely: "If you want to go, go! Go and you can sell fish at Kensington Market. You're good for nothing else."

The National Theatre School of Canada hardly knew how to cope with him. He was already practising his belief in the dictum "Laugh and you are free."

Once he began his professional career, it was evident that his genius would upset veterans, especially stars who were unaccustomed to be challenged by a novice for applause.

His greatest early fame came at the Shaw Festival where his genius flowered in English farce, his one-man *Gunga Heath*, and climaxed with his unforgettable Cyrano de Ber-gerac. (The most heartbreaking Cyrano I ever saw, bar none other on stage or film.) Robin Phillips complained that Lamberts' Cyrano was a disaster with the rhymed verse, but the genius director failed to see that the essence of this Cyr-ano was a poetic heart, a child's innocent heart trapped in an ungainly body. The romance of this Cyrano was a tragic adventure into unrequited love and gallantry.

The late Jennifer Phipps (one of the great instinctive actresses) and Barry MacGregor, an underrated supporting actor in several first-rate theatre companies, both colleagues of Lamberts at the Shaw Festival, recognized this genius. MacGregor was quite content to be Lamberts' "feed," that is, the one who is a straight man or foil to the comic half of a duo. MacGregor knew better than to get in the way of Lamberts' inspired lunacy. He knew that the genius could stop a show with spontaneous repartee with an audience member and then return to the exact spot he had stopped the show and resume as if nothing untoward had occurred. "On stage, he would mutter directions under his breath. He knew what he wanted. He had a quality with an audience that was absolutely unique."

Lesser actors resented these star moments. Gossip grew about Lamberts' demons, one reportedly being his monstrously temperamental ego. Lamberts became *persona non grata* across the country. So, he had no other choice but to leave for more congenial shores.

My regret is that he left so late. Canada clearly did not know how to handle him. It had no place for his genius.

But the United States did—on Broadway and in Pittsburgh, where he got to play roles he would never had been given in his home country. Strangely, gossip about his egomania did not pollute his reputation in the States.

Was it because that country knows how to handle genius better?

Lamberts died too soon. But even as he suffered incredible pain from cancer, he didn't complain of his affliction. He didn't deem it necessary to tell me in our final brief exchange of emails that he was dying. Suddenly I happened on an obituary notice in a Canadian newspaper. Characteristically, it contained vitriol from a famous artistic director who claimed to have made Lamberts a star and who sounded off on Lamberts' egotistical misconduct. How wrong, how egregiously mistimed, but how characteristic of this country that cannot abide real genius when it seemingly intrudes on art and life.

Genius, any small-minded man should know, is not really an intrusion on anything. It is a whole-scale revolt that enlarges both art and life.

PART TWO

PLAYS AND
PLAYWRIGHTS

Bad Poets,
Good Playwrights?

BAD POETS CAN MAKE GOOD PLAYWRIGHTS—HAROLD PINTER, for example—but good playwrights need not be good poets, although it is thrilling to have a balance of poet and playwright (as in the cases of Shakespeare, John Millington Synge, and Tennessee Williams).

Shakespeare's case is particularly interesting. He belongs to an era where language was valued in itself. People went to *hear* a play—which implies that rhetorical theatre and poetic drama could have had magical or medical power for them.

Alas, too many contemporary playwrights and directors treat words as if they were the enemy of drama. The modern trend has been towards something called "physical theatre," where movement, choreography, videography, *et cetera* displace the importance of language. Robert Wilson, Robert Lepage, Maria Abramovic, and the like do create memorable stage imagery, but their sort of theatre pushes into realms of optical illusion or surrealism. Some of this imagery has an undeniable poetic beauty—but a beauty that can be replicated through a Xeroxing of production concept and special effects. In their cases, the audience seeks *visual* pleasure and poetry, and the auditory aspect of theatre, along with the mystery of the actor, is diminished.

Robert Lepage's
Theatre of Technology

ℯ

HE HAS BEEN CALLED "A MAGICIAN OF IMAGES," WITH A SPECIAL theatrical language, "a visual, sound-based, musical, and only incidentally text-based language." Suitcases, backpacks, duffle bags, shoes, glass balls, flasks, baskets, dolls, cigarettes, puppets, screens, mats, mirrors, computers, cameras, microphones, and video screens populate his productions, forcing actors to co-exist with these objects. And it is true that he creates fascinating, sometimes complex images, in which lighting becomes part of the emotion of a scene, where photography is a metaphor related to memory, and where video divides space into different facets of the same reality, creating a visual architecture, as it were.

But is this enrichment ... or a confusion of realms ... or both?

He believes that "Theatre is about writing." He believes people tend not to realize this. "Writing is an ongoing process. It's full of unfinished sentences, crossed-out words."

But isn't this merely demarcating a boundary between process and product? Isn't rehearsal an ongoing process? Isn't it full of unfinished business, rejected choices, repetitions with modifications? Isn't it possible to rehearse a play endlessly, without having to worry about opening a production? Many East European theatre companies subscribe to this view of endless rehearsal. Some of them have been known to boast about rehearsing a play for almost a year.

We do not need to be narcotized by the morphine of academics to understand that Lepage makes a strong case for theatre as a contemporary visual language. He seems to be suggesting that we cannot practise theatre today as if there had been no photography, cinema, computers, the Internet, virtual environments, and the evolution of visual arts. He saturates the stage with heterogeneity. His champions assert that he "stages" technology, dramatizing it.

So, where does this leave the actor?

He is subordinated to technology, to the machinery that is present on stage. In other words, he is dehumanized.

Lepage would possibly argue that, on the contrary, the actor is doubled or tripled by some of the stage technology because his very form is multiplied by visual effects, such as the split-screen technique. Just as an audience is when it gazes at the visual image, drawing itself into the image's centre.

And yet, it is also possible to argue that the actor and audience are so immersed in the image that they become its prisoner.

This is not to deny Lepage's huge successes—especially his Stratford *Coriolanus* (2018), the most richly filmic, passionate version that festival has ever seen. It narrated its story through projected *trompe l'oeil* imagery, live video, sliding diorama-like boxes and panels that expanded or contracted like equivalents of cinematic pans, tracking shots, close-ups, and letter-box effects. But it also had an excellent cast of charismatic actors and an actress (Lucy Peacock) of bravura force.

Lepage's form of meta-theatre is fascinating, but its evident limits are equally fascinating.

A great play can have an after-life because of its language, characters, and exploration of story-telling. Can a theatre built primarily on technological effects have such an after-life?

Telling the Story

WE OFTEN HEAR DIRECTORS AND ACTORS CLAIM THAT THEIR primary focus is on telling the story clearly. They point to Shakespeare's ability to transcend his subplots and various plot complications in the pursuit of a clear story with compelling characters. But Shakespeare was a rare genius who could engross, challenge, question, and control his audience. So, when directors instruct their casts on opening night to just go out and tell the story, they sound rather glib. Whatever the motive and inspirations for Shakespeare's stories, society and the theatre have changed radically since his day, so is it really possible to tell his stories simply and clearly? What is the contemporary importance of ideas such as the Great Chain of Being or the Divine Right of Kings or of Prospero's magic? Does the subject of witchcraft have the same impact on a modern Western audience as it did in Shakespeare's time? No story can ever tell itself. Isn't the story subject to the director's approach and the cast's interpretation? Every production inevitably highlights certain passages of text, and although theatre does not limit an audience's gaze the way an edited film does, it nevertheless can impose a director's context or concept, or hinge on famous actors' interpretations of the principal roles.

As audiences, we all bring our conscious or subconscious biases to a story in the theatre, and for a production to tell the story clearly, it would mean that the production would have to communicate itself around those biases with as few meddling filters as possible. Moreover, telling a story means sharing a story, and the success of the telling depends on the openness of the sharing both in terms of what is offered by the production and how it is received by the audience.

Filthy Shakespeare

DESPITE MY DEEP-SEATED DISTASTE FOR MANY ACADEMIC writers, I know that there are brilliant scholars whose understanding of Shakespeare and the human condition add significantly to our appreciation of Shakespeare's genius. Such writers remove Shakespeare from the classroom and the long shadows of puritanism to show how rich and complex the poet-playwright was in his craft and art.

In his sonnets, Shakespeare was capable of obscene wordplay, entangling his name in the sexual act with men and women. Sonnet 135, for instance, contains multi-layered puns on male and female sex organs, sexual desire, and the sex act itself. The first 126 sonnets express his homoerotic love for a handsome young aristocrat (probably Henry Wriothesley, 3rd Earl of Southampton), while Sonnets 127–152 are about his adulterous affair with a mysterious woman who, in turn, was having an affair with Shakespeare's adored young man. Sonnet 151 describes a battle between the poet and his penis.

I wish our high schools would catch up with Shakespeare's bawdy irreverence in his plays. Students tend to giggle at Lady Macbeth's line "I have given suck and know/ How tender 'tis to love the babe that milks me," and they get a huge kick out of the drunken Porter's references to the good and bad effects of drink on a man's sexual urges: "it provokes the desire, but it takes away the performance." But do they really know Shakespeare's bawdiness—the multiple sexual puns lurking in his vast body of work?

Teachers and their students should rush out and get a copy of Pauline Kiernan's *Filthy Shakespeare,* a work of scholarship (as one critic has claimed) "dressed up, with brilliant design, as titillation." I have been studying Shakespeare's texts a long time, but I did not know the *extent* to which his biography and literary oeuvre were drenched in raunchiness. Specialists have known of the sexual play on his name—William Shakespeare being a double sexual pun: "Will" meant prick, cunt, and sexual desire, while "Shakespeare" connoted masturbation because to shake one's spear meant manual phallic stimulation or jerking off (in contemporary speech). But there is so much more in the work: a veritable encyclopaedia of saucy filth.

Shakespeare appealed as much to groundlings as to courtiers in his wordplay, as Kiernan scrupulously notes. A bank in his day meant a brothel district, and a famous or infamous one that lay around the corner from the Globe Theatre was called The Cardinal's Hat, named for the colour of the tip of an engorged penis. Kiernan notes that "tongue" could mean a clitoris, "noon" an erect penis at its height, and "slippery" a term to describe a bisexual. People in Shakespeare's day were skilled listeners (who went to hear a play, two hundred of them available every season), and they could decode a sexual pun instantaneously.

In his plays, words are concrete, physical, but there was subtlety—as, for example, in *Love's Labour's Lost,* one of the most eloquent examples of a feast of language. Kiernan selects a short passage between Biron and Rosaline to illustrate a witty linguistic contest, with sex as its subtext:

> *Biron*: Did not I dance with you in Brabant once?
> *Rosaline*: Did not I dance with you in Brabant once?
> *Biron*: I know you did.
> *Rosaline*: How needless was it then
> To ask the question!
> *Biron*: You must not be so quick.
> *Rosaline*: 'Tis long of you, that spur me with such
>   questions.
> *Biron*: Your wit's too hot, it speeds too fast, 'twill tire.
> *Rosaline*: Not till it leave the rider in the mire.

The subtext comes throbbingly to life with the words "dance," "quick," "spur," "wit's," "speeds," "rider," and "mire." After Kiernan's paraphrase in which she explains all the sexual meanings, she asserts that "This plethora of punning and wordplay reflects a central theme of the play—that sexual language is used as a substitute for sexual action."

Our contemporary dramatists could learn useful lessons in sexual double-entendres, and our students may be hard-pressed to keep their hormones in check as they learn things about cunning sexual wordplay.

And yet, there is an important caveat that could be laid against Kiernan's book, and it is one that eminent scholar Stanley Wells articulates in *Shakespeare, Sex and Love*. While perusing Kiernan's book, I did feel that there were several occasions when the author was deliberately exaggerating Shakespeare's "filthy" language and was distorting his wordplay by insistently pornographic paraphrase, losing the subtlety or obliquity—a point that Wells makes explicit.

Wells asserts that Shakespeare's bawdy is "often indirect, metaphorical, or allusive. Only at its least subtle does it use blunt, unequivocal terms of sexual description, the familiar four-letter words." His explanation is something professional actors and directors should learn as a radical wisdom. Too many of them cannot allow sexual wordplay to unfold without underlining the bawdy with grossly explicit physical gestures that quickly become clichés of porn. Amusing, perhaps, to the wildly innocent, but tiresome to those who know that Shakespeare was not a foul-mouthed stand-up comic in the Andrew Dice Clay or Lisa Lampanelli mould.

Chekhov's Birch Trees

IT IS NOT CUSTOMARY FOR EVEN THOSE SATURATED IN THEATRE to reflect on Chekhov's birch trees in *The Three Sisters*. My own moment of awareness came while reading Tadashi Suzuki's *Culture Is the Body*, a collection of his theatre writings. Suzuki has explored Noh, Kabuki, and Greek drama, Shakespeare's classics, and modern masters such as Chekhov and Beckett. As a thinker and practitioner, he has a powerful influence on theatre internationally. His book (a compilation of his major writings over forty years) compels us to think about what we often take for granted in the theatre, and shows that, when we do think, we can often be surprised.

Chekhov's celebrated play is about three sisters living in a countryside, who find their daily routines so boring that they develop a fantasy about returning to Moscow, their home place. Masha, the second oldest sister, is married but falls in love with a captain from their late father's regiment. The oldest sister, Olga, is a spinster who complains daily of her stressful life as a schoolteacher. The youngest sister, Irina, marries a baron. The three sisters eventually submit to events, abandon their fantasy, and resign themselves in despair to continuing their mundane life in the countryside. In the final scene, after the regiment has left to the music of a military band, the sisters emerge from a grove of white birches and speak their final lines. But the audience discovers that the three have created a new fantasy—an expression of their collective wills to work while Time passes. They recognize that they will die and be forgotten, and yet their suffering will be turned to joy for those living after them. Irina believes that there will be an end to their misery and that they will know why we (humans) suffer. Olga fashions a vision of happiness and peace on earth.

Suzuki correctly challenges the idea that this final scene is evidence of modern realism. He recognizes the conventions of Chekhov's day, but he maintains that Chekhov knew full well that his characters were not everyday people offering a slice of life.

How could he be wrong, especially when he deftly presents the premise of this play: three adult sisters (two of whom are unmarried) living together in one house? The married one lacks a healthy intimacy with her husband, so she does little other than read books, whistle idly, and ends up having an affair. "It's hard to believe," contends Suzuki, "that these three sisters would walk out into a garden together, stand next to a group of birch trees and cry, 'We must live.'"

The birch trees, therefore, are not an example of realism or naturalism. They exist in order to engage an audience's imagination in the quest for plumbing the human psyche.

Following Suzuki, we must ask ourselves whether the birch trees are indispensable to Chekhov's symbolic meaning. Is there a different way to stage the final scene, without the birch trees, and would a director's choice of options galvanize the statements of the three sisters?

The Curious Case of Ibsen

HENRIK IBSEN WROTE PLAYS PRIMARILY FOR THE MIDDLE class. His themes usually issued from family and married life, as in *A Doll's House, Ghosts, Hedda Gabler, The Wild Duck,* and *Lady from the Sea*. In each of these plays, an individual contests a difficult domestic situation: Nora's dramatic exit from a stifling marriage to a husband who will not allow her to be herself—very much like their 19th century society that denies women autonomy; Mrs. Alving who tries to shield her sensitive son Oswald from the truth about his dead father and the disease that will drive the son mad; Hedda's obsessive neurotic need for freedom and power in a conventional, hypocritical society; Gregers Werle's attempts to root out an unhealthy system and destructive family secrets; and the intensely conflict-ridden frustrations of Ellida who has to choose between her dull husband and the man who was once the love of her life.

All these plays have a realistic surface and characters with highly credible psychological distempers that make fitting subjects for Freudian analysis. However, they also transcend realism by poetic emblems, ensuring that Ibsen's appeal goes beyond realism. In fact, what makes Ibsen such a major, significant playwright is the fact that his realism has a built-in scepticism and an idealism that often creates its own sort of poetry. Even his primarily social or political plays (*An Enemy of the People, Pillars of Society,* or *Rosmersholm*) have tropes that simply take off, carrying idealism to poetic heights.

Such thoughts came to mind as I watched Carey Perloff's production of *John Gabriel Borkman* at the Stratford Shakespeare Festival, Ontario in the summer of 2016. It was clear that Ibsen was pushing deeper and deeper into symbolism. There were clearly two cages in the story: one being the dreary room in which Borkman paced like a restless wolf; the other being the cage in which his soul seemed trapped. Ibsen was obviously suggesting a wintry landscape of the soul in this drama by virtue of setting the action in winter, with snow and ice representing symbolic emblems for psyches, such as JGB's and that of his chilly wife Gunhild who has rejected him in every manner possible. But there is also coldness in other characters: JGB's son Erhart is cold towards his parents; Gunhild's twin sister Ella maintains a cool façade to conceal for a time her bitterness towards JGB for having ditched her in favour of furthering his political ambition. And there is a dramatic scene near the end where JGB, caught up in the fantasy of his "inexhaustible, bottomless, endless kingdom," trudges crazily in the snow, Ella behind him, to the edge of a steep mountain, where he dies after a heart attack. His final dialogue with Ella is shot through with a wild poetry because of his disturbed mind and soul that react to the icy wind as if it were a greeting from "captured spirits." But mixed in with his delusion of a grand ambition is his attempt to express his love for Ella. And the result is an outpouring that comes from a deeply disturbed psyche, but an outpouring with highly charged emblems of his cold, dark kingdom—in other words his maddened soul.

So, one of the lessons that Ibsen teaches all aspiring actors, directors, and playwrights is a lesson about size or dimension. There is no question that he presents many sides of an argument or discussion within a play. There is no doubt that with him, "realism has everything to do with thinking"—as the great acting teacher Stella Adler commented. And there is no doubt that Ibsen elected prose over poetry in his plays—without denying poetic symbols and moods. But his quest for truth in a person also meant that he liked to go bigger in his realism. And the corollary was to create something that would make his audience bigger as well.

Size sometimes matters.

Opening Night of
The Glass Menagerie
on Broadway
e

It was Laurette Taylor's return to the Broadway stage after more than a decade. Booze had taken over her life to the point where she and a gin bottle became inseparable. Desperate for money and an effective comeback, she seemed to take to the role of Amanda Wingfield with especial understanding and feeling, though a bucket was kept in the wings so this "alcoholic of alcoholics" could throw up.

There was thunderous applause for her first entrance, and this threw her off-course, causing her to jump into the second act. However, through the patient, understanding effort of Eddie Dowling, playing her restless son Tom, she was brought back safely into the first act. Taylor played through a fog, as it were, giving one of the greatest theatrical performances while also retching violently in the wings between her scenes.

Taylor's Amanda Wingfield was a life-size incarnation of panic, hysteria, desire, and a frustrated heart. Her performance almost obliterated that of anyone else on stage.

The cast took twenty-four curtain calls, with Taylor (according to her biographer Marguerite Courtney) "holding out the ruffles of the ancient blue taffeta as though she might break again into the waltz of her girlhood." She cried, but as soon as the curtain descended for the final time, she admitted to not remembering anything.

"Does it look like a success?" she asked Dowling as she threw her arms around him. Told she must be deaf for not hearing the massive applause, she brushed that aside: "Oh, don't give me all that nonsense! Why wasn't there some reaction to my funny lines?"

Edward Albee, R.I.P.

ce

SEPTEMBER 16, 2016 AND EDWARD ALBEE HAS DIED AT 88. America's greatest playwright after Eugene O'Neill, Tennessee Williams, Arthur Miller, and Tony Kushner. As usual, misunderstood and misjudged by inferior critics, many of whom also misjudged Williams and Miller. Sometimes he did compound this problem with critics by a stubborn Sphinx-like silence or deliberate ambiguity about the "meaning" of one of his difficult plays—the most perplexing being *Tiny Alice*. For this serious formulation of mystery for its own sake, he was sometimes excoriated by critics.

If I were to try and single out a single wrenching theme from his overall work, it would be existential loneliness, the feeling of being an outsider alienated from the rest of society or even from life itself. I remember my excitement at discovering *The Zoo Story* in 1962 when I was an undergraduate. This one-act play, with only two characters, touched a nerve. As a teenage actor, I identified with Jerry, the disturbed, acutely lonely young man, whose complaints about the world and God ran parallel with mine at the time. I related to his sensitivity, his bitterness, melancholy, need to connect with anyone or anything, be it vegetable, mineral, animal or human. In fact, Jerry seems to think of man as nothing more than an animal with instinctive drives. He mocks Peter, the married man, and goads him into fighting over a park bench, even to the point of engineering his own suicide. I relished the play's rude humour, spontaneously hysterical eloquence, and its keen intuition of despair.

Later, as a teacher of English who also ran a Drama Club, I staged both *The Zoo Story* and *The American Dream* at a Catholic high school in Montreal, shocking some of the nuns and a tall, eccentric spinster English teacher whose appreciation for theatre began and ended with Shakespeare. She could recite practically the entire text of any Shakespearean play she ever staged, revelling in her talent for making expensive costumes that usually sat awkwardly on her teenage cast. In terms of theatricality, she was closer to Earle Grey than Peter Brook, to put it most charitably. I noticed her occasional shudder at Albee's vulgarities, and her utter displeasure at having to share the theatre auditorium with a colleague (me) who did not allow his love of Shakespeare to shove aside the best of contemporary dramatists. But even she could not discount the satire of Albee's one-act vaudeville sketch, *The American Dream*, that poked grotesque fun at the middle-class and its superficial values.

In certain ways Albee's plays—major and minor—were more European than American because of their symbolic devices, candid carnality, and debts to Strindberg, Beckett, and Ionesco. Although not a poet in the theatre the way Williams was, Albee conveyed a sharp sense of existential loneliness and the paranoid terror it could breed. Like Williams, he recognized that we are all condemned to solitariness inside our own skins, and like both Williams and Miller, he made room for cries of the heart. His scaffolding was not as strong as Miller's, nor was his moral dialectic, but he took the measure of complacency, tattered hopes, useless recriminations, desperate needs. And he gave the modern theatre great roles that invited great performances.

PART THREE

LIVING THEATRE

Being Part of Living Theatre

THE PRACTISING CRITIC SHOULD ALWAYS BE—BUT RARELY is—considered part of the theatre.

The critic is customarily treated as an enemy of the theatre. Usually by the public, often by the profession itself. If he offers wholesale, indiscriminate praise, he is embraced with devotion. If he holds productions and their craftsmen to high artistic standards, he doesn't generally win approval.

Almost more than any performing art, theatre is the case of the ailing ego. Directors don't want to be held accountable for their inane concepts. Actors want critics to kiss their ass, hold their hand, or camouflage their sterile mediocrity.

More often than not, neither directors nor actors have enough faith in themselves to enjoy the comfort of something greater than themselves.

And similar charges can also be laid against critics—if they act like star-fuckers or treat theatre as personal amusement and balm for their delicate egos. There are some critics who measure their value according to the number of friends they can make in the theatre.

This attitude reeks of almost obscene vulgarity because it betrays a desperate need to be liked. Not loved. There is a vital difference.

Love enters the scene only when questions of deadline, popularity, and reward are beside the point.

Being liked is measured on a congeniality scale.

Being loved is measured by the extent to which a critic deepens his craft, avoids exploitation (of himself and of the art), and writes both for himself and for posterity—though he will not be alive when "posterity" materializes.

Theatre as an
Academic Practice
ℰ

As a graduate student in Montreal (aeons ago), I had
wanted to do a thesis on Olivier's magnificently operatic
Othello (which I had seen multiple times on film), but aca-
deme decreed that such a topic was not really within the
bounds of a *literary* thesis. The acting head of the English
department (who excelled, indeed, revelled in minute research
on the most arcane subjects in Shakespeare) felt that my topic
belonged to theatre or film studies rather than literature. I
naively switched topics to an academic exploration of *Hamlet*—more precisely the topics of Extravagance, Mediocrity,
and fire imagery in the tragedy, as a way of showing that the
Prince was not simply a victim of melancholy but of black
bile or *choler adust*. I did an enormous amount of research
into such things as Renaissance psychology and philosophy,
in addition to covering medical treatises by Galen, Levinus
Lemnius, and others. My selection of *Hamlet* was a daft
decision because I soon learned that virtually every professor of English is convinced that he has the only justifiable
interpretation of the tragedy. All other contrary interpretations are beyond the pale for these dogmatic Shakespearean
authorities. Nevertheless, I persisted. The voluminous
breadth of my scholarly background reading (every major
critic up to 1970 from A.C. Bradley, Lily B. Campbell, E.K.
Chambers, Maurice Charney, Harold Goddard, and W.H.

Clemen to Maynard Mack, Salvador de Madriaga, Peter Phialas, A.P. Rossiter, Caroline Spurgeon, E.E. Stoll, E.M.W. Tillyard, Mark Van Doren, G. Wilson Knight, and J. Dover Wilson) should have been enough, as one of my professors joked, to merit the degree automatically.

My M.A. oral defence was entertaining because it gave me the opportunity to keep silent watch from the sidelines, as it were, as various professors argued their competing views of the play. Their heated and often irrelevant and *ad hominem* exchanges done, they finally got around to passing my thesis, but not before one or two of them took credit for *my* scrupulous research. One of the consequences of this experience was my inveterate post-graduate hostility to desiccated academic theory and most scholarly writing that fattens on what it feeds—mainly huge clumps of jargon and mounds of pompous intellectual claims.

As a literary and theatre scholar, I could not afford, of course, to shut out all academic writing, but I practised the craft of critical discretion, selecting those writers who wrote in clear English and who didn't lose themselves in labyrinthine thickets of hifalutin post-modernism. So, it became relevant to me to separate the likes of Harold Bloom, James Shapiro, Stephen Greenblatt, Alexander Leggatt, and Marjorie Garber from hordes of lesser others who seem to suffer from an inordinate passion for the deliberately obscure.

As I moved deeper into theatre studies, I moved deeper into less academic, but far more useful writing. I devoured books on theatre by James Agate, J.C. Trewin, Alan Dent, Felix Barker, Eric Bentley, Peter Brook, Jonathan Miller, Ronald Eyre, Michael Benthall, Walter Kerr, Jan Kott,

Kenneth Tynan, Robert Brustein, Charles Marowitz, John Lahr, Simon Callow, *et al.* And I noticed how vivid, how penetrating, how enlightening these writers were in their distinctive prose styles. It wasn't a matter of agreeing with all their views on actors, directors, or texts. In fact, I often disagreed with them, but they all excited my lust for theatre, even when individual actors, directors, or playwrights disappointed me. Perhaps because most of them had had some practical experience in various capacities and in varying degrees with professional theatre. And it was no surprise that those who had been inside the profession often had the best insights into the processes of acting and directing.

Let the academic masters of the prolix proliferate in their desperate need to publish or perish. Let them continue to pollute literature. They remain largely irrelevant, except to their own incestuous breed.

Give me James Agate on Rachael or Sarah Bernhardt, Peter Brook on the Empty Space, Jonathan Miller on the after-life of plays, Walter Kerr and Kenneth Tynan on almost any theatrical subject, John Lahr on Tennessee Williams, and Simon Callow on Orson Welles or Charles Laughton, and I can fill many a month with voluptuous reading pleasure.

Alas, some contemporary directors have become infected by the worst academic theories, and proceed to cut, trim, and squeeze even the classics into their narrow Procrustean moulds. But not before delivering the most pompous defences of their idiosyncratic productions. Intelligence is always admirable but too much cerebration can defeat theatre.

Actors, too, can ruin performances by an excess of thought, especially influenced by extravagant theories.

Stage interpretation is not about proving a thesis or theory. Hamlet's thinking too purposefully on action should be left to his own story. It is not necessary or even advisable for Thespis to evolve into Derrida or Baudrillard, Artaud or Grotowski.

PTSD in Shakespeare

Directors can't resist the urge to assert the stage
as the rightful place to warm the latest rage.
Hamlet has been made to subsist too long
on foreign translation and E. Jones' song,
where kinky Oedipus without tender art
usurps Shakespeare's genius to mend the heart.
'Tis the way of the world to show so bold
how to modernize Bradley, to whom it is cold.
Brave Macbeth struggling in the storms of fate,
greatly falling with his sword to a bad state,
what bosom beats not with pity for the cause
when PTSD today has set its own laws.
Any hideous action by psychiatry is viewed,
leaving every tragic figure unduly subdued.
Who sees them acted, Richard Three or Henry Five,
ignobly vain yet often tear-jerkingly alive,
their native worth noted and approved,
show we have new reasons to be moved.
As tyrants no more their great savage natures keep,
foes to virtue now wonder why their hard hearts weep.
It's not all for love, the world's well lost,
psychiatry's got everyone tempest tost.

Sex in Theatre Biography

Sᴇxᴜᴀʟ ɢᴏssɪᴘ ʜᴀs ᴀɴ ᴏʙᴠɪᴏᴜs sᴀʟᴀᴄɪᴏᴜs ᴀᴘᴘᴇᴀʟ ɪɴ biographies. Theatre biographies—at least in Canada—tend to be dry, colourless, unexciting, aimed more at academics who keep score for Canadian content and nationalism. The best theatre biographies are of non-Canadians, such as Eleanora Duse, Sarah Bernhardt, John Barrymore, Laurence Olivier, Alec Guinness, Michael Redgrave, Vivien Leigh, Ralph Richardson, *et cetera*. Is it because of their enormous theatrical gifts, glamour, exceptional experiences on and off stage, personality and temperament, or the sheer drama of their private lives? What role does sex play in these biographies? Should it even matter?

There are a few theatre biographers who shrink away from sexual revelations because they think the theme is irrelevant or distracting. But is this true? It certainly would be if the biography is mainly concerned with the boudoir rather than with the acting. When I read the sloppy writing of Darwin Porter and Danforth Prince—as in their biography of Peter O'Toole, who is boldly proclaimed a "Hellraiser/Sexual Outlaw/Irish Rebel" in the subtitle—I am invited to wallow in the heft of salacious gossip, contrived dialogue (most of it unbelievable as real-life quotation), irrelevant anecdotes, and sheer kiss-and-tell vulgarity. The rear cover blurbs say as much: "Princess Margaret was

insatiable. Calling every day, couldn't get enough of me."
(Peter O'Toole); "My greatest sexual thrill involved going
to bed with Peter and some girl at the same time." (Richard
Burton); "If there's not a dame on this set I can't screw, my
name's not Peter O'Toole." (O'Toole); "Katharine Hepburn
called me a pig and a drunk ... I told her that one night with
me would cure her of her lesbianism." (O'Toole). The quotations accurately portend a racy, gossipy tabloid biography.
But apart from establishing the randy zestfulness of the
actor, what does this show about his acting?

Sheer masculinity off or on stage can be boring. Muscles
and cock are simply muscles and cock. It doesn't take any
particular genius to score in bed. Money and fame, drugs and
booze, stamina and orgasmic power are practical lures of a
Casanova—as are simple opportunity and timing. But just
being an attractive stud—straight, gay, or bisexual—does
not have any bearing on acting ability. (If it did, every *Playgirl*
hustler or model would be a great stage actor.) Did Peter
O'Toole's or Richard Burton's high success rate as lovers
translate into high success as actors? And if so, how? And
was the correlation between their sexual identities and acting personalities the same on stage as on screen? Why or
why not? Gossip-ridden biographies never address these
questions, much less offer answers.

In other cases, there are interesting issues that can be
raised by sexual revelation, provided the quality of writing
in the biography is superior. For instance, in the case of Alec
Guinness, the married man and father with Catholic guilt,
who led a secret life as a gay, or in the wrenching case of
Michael Redgrave, also married and a father, who did not
allow his secret bisexuality and taste for rough gay sex

interfere with his sensitive stage work. Or, most touchingly, the case of Vivien Leigh, the manic depressive given to sordid episodes of nymphomania, who managed to preserve her mask of elegance, grace, beauty, and style while hovering close to complete breakdown. How did she manage to give her great performances while trying desperately to cope with her deep psychic disturbances? A great biographer would be able to show the bearing of sexuality on theatrical performance.

Sex is important in theatre biography if there is a significant link between sexual identity or conflict and theatre identity—as in the case of our own late, lamented William Hutt. Here was a theatre giant of enormous skill and stature, yet one who bubbled for much of his early life with Angst about a sexual ambiguity that put him at odds with religion, family, and society. Knowing how often or the manner in which he engaged in intercourse is hardly relevant to his acting. However, it is instructive to know how his bisexuality coloured some of his best performances, adding layers of complexity to the portraits. One of these layers was a gentle melancholy that was deeply affecting and that transcended his technical expertise. However, in customary Canadian fashion, his private life held a discreet, tasteful veil over its more sordid episodes—leaving him a strong, worthy Canadian icon but with far less mass appeal as a subject for sensationally lurid biography. Hutt was an acting icon—not a poster boy for a particular sexual preference.

Feeling Responsible
for the Theatre

Ce~

STELLA ADLER CONTENDED THAT ENGLISH ACTORS FEEL responsible for the theatre—unlike their American counterparts. In the main, these actors do not abandon the stage merely for lucrative careers in film or television. This was certainly true of the great ones of the 20th century: John Gielgud, Ralph Richardson, Michael Redgrave, Laurence Olivier, and Paul Scofield. Olivier, of course, was the exception: he had a first-rate film career, and he was a matinee idol because of his roles in *Wuthering Heights, Rebecca, Pride and Prejudice, That Hamilton Woman, Henry V,* and *Hamlet.* But he sacrificed a multi-million-dollar film contract to return to the theatre and become the utter *non-pareil* of stage actors, as well as an artistic director who gave entrée to a new generation of outstanding players, such as Lynn Redgrave, Michael Gambon, Frank Finlay, Robert Stephens, Derek Jacobi, Ian McKellan, Albert Finney, Maggie Smith, Geraldine McEwan, Dennis Quilley, Colin Blakely, *et cetera.*

Other great actors did abandon the theatre for money, but most returned to the stage from time to time. Alec Guinness, perhaps a more naturally cinematic actor than Olivier, realized that film was more congenial to his talent, but even he scored theatrical triumphs intermittently throughout his long career. Richard Burton was a different case—an actor with one of the greatest voices in the history of theatre, a burning intelligence, and a heavy dramatic presence. But he succumbed to the lure of Elizabeth Taylor and the jangle of Hollywood coins—yet not before he had fulfilled his obligation to be a standard bearer, to continue a tradition of playing small and large roles in the classics, of doing his Hamlet, Othello, Iago, Henry V, and Coriolanus. In fact, Burton did two stage Hamlets—one in Britain and the other on Broadway to varying degrees of success.

As Stella Adler remarked: "English actors don't dare die without playing Hamlet—they don't dare! They don't dare because it is England, and England has this tradition. That is the measure for the English."

The American actor has no such responsibility and does not see any need to discover one. Theatre becomes merely a conduit to film or television. If you think this is an overgeneralization, name me the American exceptions beyond Kevin Spacey and Al Pacino. After Marlon Brando went to Hollywood, he never returned to the stage. He became a brand, a great one, but his astounding portraits on film far outnumbered the ones he had created on stage.

There are major film stars who have made infrequent returns to Broadway, mainly in special or carefully managed circumstances. Katharine Hepburn, Robert de Niro, Jack Lemmon, Meryl Streep, Jessica Lange, and a few others. Kim Stanley, Julie Harris, Maureen Stapleton, and Geraldine Page, in a sense, were never film stars, so their hearts were always in the theatre.

But where are the cases of great latter-day American actors who feel a burning, nationalistic, patriotic need to keep American theatre flourishing rather than their own bank accounts? Could they ever say with any justification that they are an integral part of a repertory system? Would they seriously fight against being typecast, of taking mighty risks in roles that run counter to their screen images? In America, you don't necessarily become famous because of versatility; you become famous for repeating yourself, for latching onto a single personality and playing it for all its worth incessantly. You become a gangster, or a sweetheart, a tart with a heart of gold, a middle-class mom, a second banana, a man of honour, a temperamental diva, a sheriff, a pop idol. And you trade in never-ending clichés of speech and acting.

And given the crass state of most film criticism, the public never learns anything appreciably significant about great acting. The American actor learns to wear a single mask and this mask becomes his face for as long as the public and critics accept.

When American actresses begin to age, the mask sits uneasily, so the actresses resort to plastic surgery. They get a new cosmetic mask, which is stitched onto their natural face. When these actresses have scenes in which they look into a mirror, what do they really see? Do they see the character they are playing or do they try to count new lines, new age spots, new sagging skin?

Is There an Objective
Standard of Taste?

WHEN PLAYWRIGHT SARAH RUHL DOGMATICALLY BUT shrewdly answered her own rhetorical question with the single word "No," she could not help but raise the entire issue of taste.

A rather well-known Canadian director (who had also been the artistic director of Young People's Theatre in Toronto) once tried to explain away a criticism I had made of a particular production (probably his, though I don't recall) as being simply "a matter of taste." I thought how curious it was for an arts insider to be so dismissive of a discriminating, even essential quality of analysis and judgment.

After all, in most instances, taste doesn't come down to preferring coffee over tea, or mango over mint. Nor is it simply the superficial matter of appreciating the sensory and sensual effects of skin or accoutrements. ("Nothing tastes as good as skinny feels"—Kate Moss.) I sympathise with those (such as Whoopi Goldberg) who feel disrespected for their peculiar taste in things ("Not everybody's going to dig what I dig, but I reserve the right to dig it!"). Well and passionately asserted, but a rather thin-skinned avoidance of matters of critical discrimination/discernment/mentorship.

There are famous witticisms about taste:

"This wallpaper is dreadful. One of us will have to go."
(Oscar Wilde)

"Egotist: a person of low taste, more interested in himself
than in me." (Ambrose Pierce)

"Whether you take the doughnut hole as a blank space or
as an entity unto itself is a purely metaphysical question and does not affect the taste of the doughnut at
all." (Haruki Murakami)

Fun but not what I mean by taste. I prefer Alexander Pope's
epigrammatic utterance in "An Essay on Criticism":

"In Poets as true Genius is but rare,
True Taste as seldom is the Critick's Share."

Pope was clearly suggesting that taste was a requisite for
critical analysis rather than a cursory value-judgment that
should be discarded with awful wallpaper or a metaphysical
doughnut. So, when in the 1980s I published rather inflam-
matory essays slamming the deficiency in taste and intelligence in Canadian theatre—with special attention to the
radical lapses in taste in John Hirsch, the patron saint of
Canadian ultra-nationalists, my crucial underpinning was
not racial, ethnic, sexual, regional, or religious. I understood
and expressed taste as an arbiter of standards, more aesthetic than political. Of course, I have preferences and biases.
Who doesn't? But I do not allow these to interfere with or
mar my engagement with a play or book or film or poem or
painting. I can simply declare my preference or bias and go
on from there to an exploration whose results I seek to share
with my audience.

On Generalizations
in the Theatre

ℯ

DAVID MAMET'S ESSAYS IN *WRITING IN RESTAURANTS* OFFER many intellectual provocations—rather like his plays and political views. In a piece entitled "Regarding *A Life in the Theater*," Mamet remarks that "at the end of a performance, or the end of a season, the only creation the performer has left is him- or herself. This, and artifacts: clippings, programs."

True enough, and something that should give pause to those who scorn critics and claim that they never read reviews. I can understand the fear of mockery or denunciation. Nobody—neither performer, nor critic—likes those things. But a generalized avoidance of reviews betrays either a lack of self-confidence or an unjustifiable arrogance. Surely it is easy to sift the wheat from the chaff. An actor should possess a fundamental intelligence that can separate the genuine critic from the false one.

Sweeping, gushing praise often betrays a lack of careful analysis by a critic. In fact, it is relatively easy to write a glowing review or a withering attack; the harder job is to offer a balanced review that takes into account what worked and what didn't in a performance.

If an actor avoids or refuses to read reviews, does this mean that he or she or the audience should be the ultimate arbiters of judgment or evaluation or response? This perspective leads to Rotten Tomatoes reviews, or thumbs-up/ thumbs-down Consumer Reports.

At an informal party after a performance of Chekhov's *The Seagull*, radically adapted and directed by Alexander Hausvater in Montreal, I complimented the lead actor for his interpretation of Konstantin (the youthful, impatient, self-defeating and somewhat childish son of Arkadina, a famous actress with a grand manner), and said that this performance was so much better than the interpretation he had given of the same role a season or two earlier at the Stratford Festival. An in-artful or, at least, an undiplomatic way of paying a compliment but my motive was positive. The actor's reaction was swift: "I never talk to anyone who does not like my performance." An equally swift response flashed in my mind: "Well, that would cut down the amount of conversation you will have in your career." But I kept the thought to myself.

Almost needless to say, that actor had a short-lived stage career, though he did become relatively famous in Canadian television. Material success; artistic decline.

There are famous stage performers ("still living" as Shakespeare's Benedick would put it) who cannot abide criticism. Evidently, they grant interviews only to journalists and critics who offer geysers of praise, however sycophantic and shallow. Such performers should be avoided like the plague because they do no service to the profession. Their narcissism serves only themselves.

But to return to Mamet. In the same essay, he quotes Sanford Meisner at the Neighborhood Playhouse School of the Theatre: "When you go into the professional world, at a stock theater somewhere, backstage, you will meet an older actor—someone who has been around awhile." Such a veteran actor will be full of tales and anecdotes about life in the theatre. He will speak to you "about your performance and the performances of others, and he will generalize to you, based on his experiences and his intuitions, about the laws of the stage. Ignore this man."

Meisner's advice is a cautionary against generalization, but it is a generalization itself. Of course, such veterans exist, and of course many actors will turn into forms of the same veteran.

The Seven Ages of Man should really be Eight. There is the age of Anecdotage.

But every professional should know that there are no such things as "laws of the stage," any more than there are laws about any performing art. Even guidelines or norms are generalizations.

If an artist expects to further his craft by following a law, he is in the wrong profession.

Laws in the arts are for commissars of culture—bureaucrats or the Poo-Bahs, characters who should rightly find themselves in an updated Gilbert and Sullivan satire.

Poetry

PART ONE

ON THE READING
OF IT

Keith Garebian reading some of his poetry at
St. Vartan's Armenian Church, adjoining St. Cuthbert's
Anglican Church, Oakville, September 2015.

Public Readings

POETRY READINGS ARE USUALLY EXCRUCIATING EXPERIENCES.

There is the mumbling poet—the sort who seems embarrassed by his own verse, and whose mumbling muffles the poetry.

There is the droning poet: the type who seems to suffer from a sleeping illness that infects the audience.

There is the dub poet: the sort whose accent and rhythm can turn verse into spoken arts exotica.

There is the academic poet: the professor whose pontifical introduction of a piece is fraught with promise that is rarely fulfilled.

There is the deconstructive or post-modernist poet: the one for whom craft is eccentricity, his aim "how not to hit the mark he seems to aim at," "how to avoid the obvious," and his technique "how to vary the avoidance." (Phrases borrowed from Robert Francis' "Pitcher"—where baseball and poetry are analogous for aberrations.)

There is the modern beat poet: the one caught in the wrong decade because he was born too late.

There is the tub-thumping poet: the one who belongs on a soap box in some park.

There is the declamatory poet: the one who ends his dramatic utterances by usually yelling out a famous literary or political name, as if the mere allusion were enough to put a seal on an awful poem. I experienced many instances of this type in Armenia, where poets from Georgia, Turkey, Iraq, Iran, *et cetera* invoked the names of Komidas or Saroyan or Siamanto as a dramatic but unearned climax.

There is the ham poet: the one who performs with melodramatic flourishes. He is not to be confused with the spoken art poet—the one who wishes to share the chemistry of poetry, with its distillates of diction, imagery, and tone.

(A sad fact about most poetry readings in North America is that the number of poetry readers is about the same as the number of poets.)

On "Direct" Readings

THERE IS A BIAS IN SOME LITERARY CIRCLES AGAINST HEIGHTENED effects in live readings. The bias is in favour of what is commonly called un-melodramatic, direct, simple readings—as if intelligent phrasing, with colourful emphases on certain words or images, or a sensitive negotiation of rhythm, or skilful modulations of tone are unfair advantages to a poet who respects and honours his craft by a high definition oral performance. There is an inordinate number of poets who claim that skilled spoken art camouflages a mediocre literary specimen. Perhaps, but only for those whose minds are a blank.

The antipathy towards effective oral readings betrays an inveterate insecurity or an insidious rivalry or jealousy. I never want to hear a poem recited as if it were a telephone directory. This is one reason I usually avoid poetry readings, where art or craft is murdered with almost obscene carelessness. Better to stay home and read the poet's book, if you think it deserves your attention. All poetry began with oral performance. Hence the *scop* or bard. There was a time when great poets were great readers. They had to be because most people could not afford to buy books, or because they lived in a predominantly oral culture where such things as voice, tone, and rhythm mattered greatly.

This is not meant to separate oral art from printed art.

The two should go together—as they always do in the greatest poems or the most memorable ones.

One more point: scrutinizing adjectives such as "unmelodramatic," "direct," and "simple" leads to the discovery that these are simply meaningless, useless buzz words. "Unmelodramatic" is a word that does not properly belong to poetry. And what does it mean to read directly or simply? Does it mean that a poet should play dumb and not have a personal point of view in his reading, that he should simply recite words as if they have no denotative or connotative or tonal significance? Does it mean that the poet should be insensitive to the intrinsic rhythm of a piece? Does it mean he should not show a way into his poem, or accent what he believes is the crux of his theme? Moreover, a good reading exposes the real tone of a poem, unhindered by inept enunciation or articulation.

The Reading Poet's Voice

IN PABLO LARRAIN'S CLEVER FILM *NERUDA*, THE FAMOUS Chilean poet's second wife, Delia, disapproves of the way in which he reads a new poem. He sounds flatly direct, almost toneless, so she urges him to use his poet's voice—the one she obviously has heard many times during his public readings. And, so, he obliges, adopting a sort of grave lyricism that too many poets confuse with sincerity.

There is voice, and then there is VOICE.

"Authors are actors, books are theatres," said Wallace Stevens, suggesting that poems can have incandescent histrionic power. He could have had dramatic monologues specifically in mind, such as those where the speaker adopts the voice of a real or imaginary person.

This is not to subscribe to a fetish of "voice" or physical presence, but rather (as Maureen N. McLane asserts in her essays in *My Poets*) "to keep alive a sonic dimension through which critical intelligence might also sound forth." Such poems involve us in the very process of their unfolding, and such poems breathe with the presence of their creators. They depend very much on accuracy of the voice being used to reveal the tone.

And even excepting the dramatic monologue, tone is crucially important. Apparently, not everyone can sense true tone, and there is a lamentable tendency for poets to

recite dully, almost in a monotone, as if they were embarrassed to reveal that their words can have a life of their own.

In these cases, is it rude to tune out, or is there a way of
administering morphine to one's self in case the pain of a
woeful reading becomes intolerable?

For Immediate Pleasure

POETRY SHOULD NOT BE BEATEN WITH A HOSE FOR US TO FIND out what it means. So believes American poet-laureate Billy Collins who in his satiric lyric "Introduction to Poetry" refers specifically to the wrong-headed teaching of Poetry in high schools because he believes (correctly) that high school is "the place where poetry goes to die." It isn't easy to count the number of English teachers who would rather not teach the genre at all. They include a few classes on Poetry because the official curriculum requires that they do. And their own lack of enthusiasm filters down to their hapless students who would rather take a course in Drama (mistakenly believing that it is empty of content) than in English, especially if it means having to cope with poems that treat clarity as if it were a major flaw in communication.

In his Introduction to *Poetry 180*, Collins cites the case of a high school (south of Chicago) to which he was invited as a featured poet. A female student handed him a copy of the school newspaper in which she had published an article containing "a memorable summary of the discomfort many people seem to experience with poetry." In her piece, the teenager admitted: "Whenever I read a modern poem, it's like my brother has his foot on the back of my neck in the swimming pool."

A succinct summary crystallized in a superb image of

deadly torture—and in the same league as Collins' image of a torturer's hose beating the meaning out of a poem.

The idea behind Collins' 180 anthology is to collect "a generous selection of short, clear, contemporary poems which any listener could basically 'get' on first hearing—poems whose injection of pleasure is immediate."

This immediate pleasure is something that echoes my own feeling about one of the primary properties of a successful poem. Keats once famously proclaimed "if poetry comes not as naturally as Leaves to a tree, it had better not come at all."

When did obscurity become a criterion for poetry?

Probably when academic poets took over most of the field and imposed their intellectual biases on others who were more naturally given to melody, rhythm, and tone.

Obscurity is not the same as difficulty.

This is what celebrated poet John Ashbery got wrong in his 2011 acceptance speech of the National Book Award Lifetime Achievement Award when he mocked the idea of accessibility as "a relatively recent requirement," proceeding to point out that accessibility was not the key in Picasso's paintings of heads with three eyes and Stravinsky's having four pianists banging out the same chord over and over in "Les Noces." Curious examples, given the fact that Ashbery was referencing painting and ballet orchestral work.

Ezra Pound, T.S. Eliot, Wallace Stevens, and Hart Crane ("the Mount Rushmore of modernism"—Collins) are difficult poets, but they are not really obscure in the sense of something wilfully perverse. They don't seek to hide meaning in a secret dark place that a reader can't discover unless he is adept at deciphering confidential codes.

Queen of the Desert

THE ONE REMARKABLE THING IN A LARGELY DREARY, pedestrian film biography of English writer/explorer/adventurer Gertrude Bell is not the desert (the movie was filmed in Jordan) or the Arabic that exquisite Nicole Kidman speaks in her dialogue with assorted Druze and Bedouin, but the overriding respect Bell pays to Persian and Arabic poetry. The film mentions the long history (thousands of years) of Persian poetry, but it doesn't go into details. There is a scene where rhymed verses from *Rubaiyat* of Omar Khayyam are recited from memory. However, two other finer moments stand out for me. One is where Bell is explaining the nature of her writing: she isn't a writer who would describe the land and whatever is part of it; rather, she asserts, she's one who would *name* things.

Isn't the very act of naming a re-enactment of the first human creation—something that would survive Cain and Abel and all the miserable consequences of Paradise Lost?

In a subsequent scene, when asked why she admires the Bedouin, she responds it is because of their freedom, dignity, and their poetry of life.

Of what contemporary Western culture can we say this with justification?

Gertrude Bell's clear-eyed vision easily and refreshingly transcends the bloated imperialism of Victorian England.

The Drama of the Adjective

THERE CAN BE DRAMA IN THE ADJECTIVE—SOMETHING FAR better than mere descriptive colour. Good poets know (often instinctively) which word should follow which word in sequence—not simply for sound but for tonal impact as well.

Alas, there seems to be a bias in contemporary Canadian poetry against the adjective. There is a widespread belief that adjectives somehow slacken the tension of a line or thought, when, in actuality, the opposite could be true. In the great canonical poets of the English language, the adjective is never exiled to the shores of the excommunicated. For example:

"Shall I compare thee to a summer's day?
Thou art more lovely and more temperate:
Rough winds do shake the darling buds of May,
And summer's lease hath all too short a date."
    (Shakespeare)

"Numb were the Beadsman's fingers while he told
His rosary, and while his frosted breath,
Like pious incense from a censer old,
Seem'd taking flight from heaven, without a death,
Past the sweet Virgin's picture, while his prayer he saith."
    (Keats)

"Than longen folk to goon pilgrimages,
And palmers for to seken straunge strondes,
To ferne halwes, couth in sondry londes." (Chaucer)

And here is Elizabeth Bishop from an era closer to our own, expressing love and fear in "Breakfast Song" about a very personal relationship with another woman:

"My love, my saving grace,
your eyes are awfully blue.
I kiss your funny face,
your coffee-flavored mouth."

The brief examples above speak more to ornamentation than to drama, but how about lines from T.S. Eliot:

"April is the cruellest month, breeding
lilacs out of the dead land, mixing
Memory and desire, stirring
Dull roots with spring rain."

Eliot's enjambments contribute to a sense that almost every thought is unfinished. Hence the lines have an intrinsic tension that makes instability a dramatic feature in the poem. Adjectives in the lines are the paint of language, but they spring surprises. It is tantamount to action painting—but with control as to how to shape what the brush has flung, smeared, or dripped on a canvas.

Benumbing Adjectives

C⌒

THERE ARE PROBABLY NOT A FEW POETS WHO HAVE BEEN criticized at some point for benumbing adjectives.

Edward Hirsch observes that many modern and contemporary poets are terrified of deep feeling, of seeming sentimental. "We live in a cool age," he asserts, then coolly cites the Turkish poet Nazim Hikmet for defying the age by his emotional excesses and "unblushing sentiment."

Referring back to my mini musing on the drama of the adjective, I offer my counter-argument to poets and critics who abhor the use of adjectives—or, to be fair, what they consider to be the use of unnecessary or superfluous adjectives in a poem.

A semi-autobiographical poem of mine recreates a traumatic incident from my Armenian father's early boyhood when he, his distraught mother, and his older sister were fleeing murderous Turks who were hell-bent on exterminating Armenians in 1915. As I wrote in a book-length memoir, *Pain: Journeys Around My Parents* (2000): "To be an Armenian in Islamic Turkey was to be the victim of a racial conspiracy. 'Either they disappear, or we do,' warned Talaat with fanatical conviction."

Fatigued and driven to desperation by starvation and cruelty, my father's mother gave her youngest daughter to a Kurdish farmer and his barren wife. The second daughter—

whose name my father couldn't remember—was abandoned not long after.

Too tired to carry the girl, his mother sat her by a tree and told her not to worry, that she would return to fetch her.

My father's final image of this nameless one was of a little girl with curly hair, crying by herself under an inhospitable tree.

This incident related to me by my father in his old age generated a second trauma—mine. I was *possessed* by this final image of an actual event, and the image of the little girl and the tree stayed in my mind for decades until the time came for me to memorialize it in a poem.

THE MOTHER WHO ABANDONED HER DAUGHTER

When she set her starving baby girl
crying under a spindly tree
with a false promise to return
she would have remembered her first cry
she would have remembered her brown eyes
a delicate crystal
her dark hair as soft as music
she would have remembered mothering
she would have remembered love.

Like the unremitting gaze of damaged children
the girl's eyes stared through tears, a bellyful of dirt
but there was no final rocking
in the awful dust, the soft smother
where bones could suffocate

after days of fire and hunger,
and the gnarled earth eating
into her mother's heart.

After she had set her starving baby girl
crying under a spindly tree,
forsaken faith in her own survival
slid closer to the slime of worms
sighed a sigh as dry as salt
her worried eyes, her open wound
blinked through insomniac hours
sewed her lips shut with sorrow
never to sing songs in summer
in her daughter's ear, never repeat
the fateful story that tree could tell.

The poem always elicits strong emotional reactions from audiences who have heard me read it aloud. However, a very (justly) celebrated poet once complained that it is too adjective-heavy and that, therefore, the reader is benumbed.

I would contend that most of the adjectives are necessary. While arguably not indispensable, "starving" and "spindly" reinforce the idea of starvation, both of the human and the vegetative, besides complementing each other as images of deprivation and want. The overwhelming sense of hunger is reinforced by the image of the "gnarled earth" eating into the mother's heart. The earth itself is starving, and the image evokes an eerie appetite, with the ground's becoming carnivorous—something that also expands the horror of the starving mother becoming food for the earth. The "delicate crystal" of the girl's eyes may seem exaggerated at first but it does suggest something delicate, fragile, and precious—as not only in terms of sight but as a tiny human life as well. (Perhaps somewhere in my subconscious was the lingering image of *Kristallnacht* [Night of Broken Glass] as well.) Moreover, and more importantly, one hopes the clusters make the lines expressive, and the adjectives are part of the texture of the lines. They also are part of an experience remembered and relived—a recuperation through words.

Not every line in a poem has to be astringently adjective-free. It is possible that some writers and critics are embarrassed by emotion—theirs and others'. There's no disputing the value of reticence or literary control in poetry—as in the examples of Elizabeth Bishop or Czeslaw Milosz—but there is also no disputing the emotive value of adjectives. Sometimes restraint can be as excessive as an adjective-laden poem. The test is in the motive and the strategic effect.

Finally, perhaps, it is a question of taste and sensibility rather than of any hard-and-fast rule. One man's benumbing can be another man's enchantment. Some poets and critics prefer the anti-lyric to the lyric. Does this mean that one mode is superior to the other? Not necessarily because it depends on the literary quality and function of each.

Shouldn't dogma be left to religion?

The "I's" Have It

ONE OF THE CURRENT BIASES IN POETRY IS TOWARDS THE USE of the pronoun "I." I can't remember exactly when this bias developed—Yeats, Ezra Pound, T.S. Eliot, and Charles Olson undoubtedly had something to do with it—but it's something that even the late bpNichol wrestled with in his ground-breaking *The Martyrology*. In Book 4, bp wrote:

> i am wary of that impulse within me
> would have it out with my i
> how can i cast out
> out of the process i must be true to
> is part of the dissolution
> the disillusionment
> create a third person when the i's can't get along?

bp contends that the "I" risks being read chiefly as a valorization of the self, although he also argues for more than one "I."

The "I" signifies subjective perception and experience. Why is it necessary to pretend that one's own viewpoint, feelings, beliefs somehow lessen the validity of a poetic response? Who, in any case, is the ultimate arbiter, the ultimate decider? A reader's own subjectivity necessarily comes into play in any reading and response to a poem. The "I" does not necessarily imply an absolute authority. I don't know of any being that can be considered such, apart from a concocted Godhead.

An "I" can be ambiguous if it radiates from a persona, because the question then is whether this "I" is the poet's own self or the invented one of his persona. The invented "I" (as opposed to the real "I") separates itself from the author in the act of creation—especially in monologues or soliloquies. Regardless, this is small reason to "de-privilege" it as a device, voice, and identity. Contemporary American poets use "I" without apology and with great finesse, as in the cases of Donald Hall (who wrote movingly of his poet-wife's death by cancer), Louise Glück (a superb channel for mythological personae), Robert Hass, Billy Collins (poet of direct engagement) and Edward Hirsch (who turned a dossier about the tragic death of his young adopted son Gabriel into a book-length elegy).

Leading poet-critic Richard Howard called Hirsch's narrative poem a peculiar elegy, "unlike anything anyone else has done, a modern poem about modern circumstances." What elevates Hirsch's poem above many other elegies is its wise movement into areas beyond grief towards what another writer has called "a subversion of decorum."

The "I's" of these superior poets have it—that genius to transform deep feeling into deep insight, and to combine the personal with the larger world outside that has shaped or charged the artist.

PART TWO

GENRES

Found Poems, Collages

FOUND POETRY NEED NOT BE MERE DOCUMENTARY MATERIAL. It isn't simply a question of finding sentences in a source and arranging them intact on the page to resemble a poem. I think of a found poem as if I had discovered a piece of driftwood on which I have used a chisel or a smaller, finer cutting instrument in order to pare away the unnecessary matter to reach a form I feel is within the wood.

Found poetry is a minor craft because the source is ready-made language. The utterances could be mere scraps, words or phrases, but the real skill in found poetry is an editing one, which implies a vision (the ability to see what could be a poem), an appreciation of a ready-made theme ("ready-made lovely matters"—Richard Lattimore), and a mission to promulgate what one has discovered before anyone else.

Collage is a more sophisticated craft. It is a layered design. Though it also borrows ready-made language and imagery, it makes the material shine anew.

Superb examples of collage in poetry: T.S. Eliot's *The Wasteland* and Peter Balakian's *Ozone Layer*. Interestingly, Balakian included Eliot in a major essay entitled "Collage and Its Discontents," using as an epigraph Eliot's lines: "From such chaotic, mish-mash potpourri/what are we to expect but poetry."

Balakian's essay (included in his anthology *Vise and Shadow: Essays on the Lyric Imagination, Poetry, Art, and Culture*) summarizes the kinetic force of a collage-work that pitches forward, resisting "linearity and formal closure," while maintaining "a desire to go beyond its own boundaries." A collage-work is "always bigger than the sum of its parts, but its parts are energized by their relationship to the other parts of the work, and so the work generates an energy and dynamism that draws the reader into a swirl or vortex of motion."

And, so, both Eliot and Balakian exercise and expand the idea of the lyric poem as "intellectual collage and repository of cultural texts and sources." (Balakian's words.) Eliot incorporates Petronius, the Bible, the Tarot, references to Chaucer, Baudelaire, Shakespeare, Milton, Ovid, Marvell, Verlaine, Tiresias, Wagner, St. Augustine, the Upanishad, Dante, *et cetera*. Balakian absorbs Armenian genocide history, memories of New York in the 1980s, the AIDS crisis, climate change, and personal history in order to bring "the pain of the past into the landscape of the present" (to quote Alfred Kazin on *Ozone Layer*), or, (as Bruce Smith puts it) to "derange history into poetry, make poetry painting, make painting culture, make culture living."

The Cento

AN ANCIENT FORM THAT TRACES ITS LINEAGE BACK TO HOMER and Virgil, the cento is more than a step or two above the found poem—although the actual lines used in the form are already found in other poets. The cento is a patchwork of quotations: that is, it is an arrangement of other poets' lines to form a new construct. In fact, the word "cento" is Latin for "patchwork." But it isn't a crazy quilt; rather, at its best, it's a deft construct, a rearrangement of borrowed lines that becomes a new poem.

For a good cento, the poet's mind must never wander across quotations. It needs to keep a firm focus on unity of theme, tone, and rhythm. A cento, it can be argued, is secondary creativity because it can only proceed from what already exists. But only God (or what we call God) creates *ex nihilo*.

A cento is a prime example of "unoriginal genius"—to borrow Marjorie Perloff's memorable phrase that is, in fact, the title of her brilliantly erudite book about an important development in recent poetry. Perloff describes this development as the wholesale citation of other people's words in order to make new works. She argues paradoxically that this "unoriginal" poetry is more accessible and, in a sense, "personal" than the hermetic poetry that came into fashion in the 1980s and 1990s.

A cento is unabashed theft that justifies itself by the end-product. In other words, the means justify the end.

It is worth remembering T.S. Eliot's statement about literary theft: "Immature poets imitate; mature poets steal; bad poets deface what they take; and good poets make it into something better, or at least something different."

More on Cento

ELIOT USED THE COLLAGE METHOD TO CONSTRUCT HIS MOST celebrated long poem, *The Wasteland*. This greatly ambitious work incorporates quotations and citations from other writers, in several languages. However, Eliot was not universally applauded for *The Wasteland*. He was severely criticized by a famous poet-editor for "an indolence of imagination" because his work declined, it was argued, into "a mere notation."

But neither *The Wasteland* nor the cento form is mere notation. Neither is merely a set of notes, though both use borrowed lines. Quotation or citation have a two-fold process: one of removal (the borrowing) and the other of grafting (the new construct). One of the purposes of the cento is a lyric or anti-lyric meditation, and it can be oblique and dense in its communication of emotion.

Interestingly, opponents of the cento object to its lack of personal emotion because almost every line is borrowed. But is this necessarily so?

A cento implies a community of sources and sharing. And as a new construct, each cento can express the constructor's emotion or feeling about a controlling theme. In other words, while the lines are borrowed, the tone or guiding feeling is the borrower's. So, for instance, a poet can construct a very effective cento about war or love or depression or art itself.

Theatre can be used as analogy. Is an actor devoid of personal emotion when he plays a role, voicing a playwright's words and used in the play's context?

Oulipo

A FORM THAT CANADIAN POET CHRISTIAN BOK HELPED popularize through his award-winning collection entitled *Eunoia* is the Oulipo, a precursor of 21st century poetics, founded in Paris in 1960 by Raymond Queneau and François Le Lionnais as an experimental literary collective formally known as *Ouvroir de littérature potentielle*, or Potential Literary Workshop (OuLiPo). The aim of this form is to invent or deploy a constraint of a formal nature in the composition of a new piece of literature. But the *potential* of the constraint is more important than the actual execution. Yet, the constraint is not some randomly chosen arbitrary rule imposed on a text; it describes itself. In other words, "a text written according to a constraint," (to quote Jacques Roubaud, one of its early practitioners) "describes the constraint."

An Oulipo, unlike a concrete poem, is primarily a literary rather than a visual form. Where a concrete poem depends on a distribution of verbal units, whether letters, morphemes, or whole words on a page, the Oulipo tends towards narrative. In fact, the collective adopted a pragmatic approach to fiction, more than to poetry, although Queneau did produce a flipbook of ten sonnets, where the fourteen lines on each page were printed on individual strips, "so that every line could be replaced by the corresponding one in any of the other poems."

Bok's *Eunoia* (purportedly seven years in the making) is a collection of chapters, each one devoted to a specific English vowel. The name for this form is "lipogram," a composition in which a certain letter of the alphabet is omitted deliberately. According to the book's rear cover: "A unique personality for each vowel soon emerges: A is courtly, E is elegiac, I is lyrical, O is jocular, U is obscene."

I essayed a poem built on the recurrence of the vowel "O" in my collection, *Blue: The Derek Jarman Poems*. My primary interest in this experiment was on the vowel sound itself as it reverberated through the temper or mores of Thatcher's England expressed in Jarman's experimental film *Jubilee*—a wildly inventive, punk-inspired apocalyptic fantasy of a moribund England.

Here is a brief sample:

Post-modern opus of punk words or songs. Gob smacking, rock faced proles, show working class oppression, comment on collapsed country's old order. Despondent youth hoot, holler, howl, or stomp on poor sods, young or old. *Mondo dolorosa*, O post-punk epoch. Porn, home movie shots of crotches, dorks, or 'pols.' Down, down, down on old pox-ridden kingdoms.

Oulipo can be a voluptuously sensuous experience for its creator, as well as for its readers. But does its system of building a poem from a pre-selected constraint constitute a serious creative limitation?

Is it merely experiment for experiment's sake? Or is it a way of raising questions about the production of meaning and of the rich possibilities and trends of language?

Japanese Death Poems

ℓ

THE APPROACH OF DEATH GIVES RISE TO THE "DEATH POEM" or *jisei*. Such a poem is often written in the very last moments of a poet's life; it is his dying song, as it were. The form and the practice of it go back centuries, beginning with early nobility and samurai to satirical death poems of later periods, involving Zen monks and haiku specialists.

In his lengthy, scholarly introduction to the anthology *Japanese Death Poems*, Yoel Hoffmann notes that, while wills left by dying Japanese dealt only with the division of property, the death poem was a sort of salutation—a formal salute, an act of politeness for the living. And another remarkable thing is that both the legal will and the death poem seemed to have been composed in an air of serenity. The poems put a calm seal on death.

When Buddhism took firm root in the nation, the prevailing tone was a resignation to the concept of fleetingness. Wilting flowers rather than corpses became common images. So, we find that the death poems of the Heian period are marked by flower imagery, indicative of changing seasons of longing and sorrow: a longing for spring after fall and winter; and sorrow that blossoming cherries endure only a brief period.

The case of samurai death poems is strikingly different. Images of swords, sliced heads, and bolts of lightning abound during war-torn periods, though the fanaticism is sometimes softened by images from nature in a traditional style of love poetry.

And then there is death poetry by Zen Buddhists, tending with natural simplicity towards inner enlightenment. Death is treated as a pseudo-problem, according to Hoffmann who cites the example of Yamamoto Ryokan (1758–1831) who said: "When you suffer a calamity—then be it so; now is the time of calamity. When you die—then be it so; now is the time to die. Thus you save yourself from calamity and death."

Serenity, tranquility, resignation. But are such states really little more than an anaesthesia of the mind and soul? An opiate?

We don't know what comes after death, so how can we be so calm in the face of the unknown unless we allow ourselves to be drugged by a philosophy or creed that promises something we wish for as an ultimate reward for our acquiescence?

Bassui Tokusho tries to be consoling when he writes:

Look straight ahead. What's there?
If you see it as it is
You will never err.

Tokusho is reputed to have taught with the voice of silence. I don't know how to unscramble the oxymoron. Yet just before he expired, he turned to the gathered crowd, repeated his dictum about silence in a *loud* voice, and only then passed away.

Some of the monks were seemingly on the verge of madness, such as Daigu Sochiku who struck his attendant on the head with writing paper before dying a day later. Or Dokyo Etan who "wrote his last words while seated in the upright Zen position. Then he put down his brush, hummed 'an ancient song' to himself, suddenly laughed out loud, and died." What could be more satirical?

On the anthology's own evidence, death poems seem to occasion weird private consolations for the dying. I quote six examples:

"When he finished [,] he raised the stick again, tapped the floor once more and cried, 'See! See!' Then, sitting upright, he died."

"He then put down his brush, yawned loudly, and died."

"When he had finished reciting it, he 'died.' After six hours, however, he revived and began preaching to the monks who had gathered around his bed."

"He wrote this poem on the morning of his death, laid down his brush, and died sitting upright."

"The sources tell us that on the day of his death, Musho summoned the other monks, arranged for his burial service, said his last words, and died sitting upright."

"He died sitting upright in a Zen position, his death poem lying beside his body."

Hoffmann comments: "Death in a Zen sitting position or death standing up was considered worthy of an enlightened person."

Is it more spiritual to die upright or horizontally? Should one's final words be quiet or loud? Should one's last breath be silent or audible? Without wishing to mock any particular deep-rooted spiritual or philosophic belief, it is still reasonable to note that the semiotics of dying breed their own satire.

Post-Holocaust Poetry

THEODOR ADORNO ASSERTED THAT THERE COULD BE NO poetry after the Holocaust: "To write poetry after the Holocaust is barbaric." A harsh, devastating generalization and over-statement that has been challenged triumphantly by such poets as Paul Celan, Irving Layton, Charles Simic, and Peter Balakian. Whether the poetry is a catalogue of horrors, souvenirs of hell, or a mirror that reflects man's most awful image is almost beside the point. History and historical atrocity are vises that grip us in the shadows of life; art (especially poetry) is a way of freeing us from that vise. Speechlessness—which is a synonym for silence—is a dastardly effect, a crippling condition that is inimical to civilization and culture.

Good poetry is not, of course, a department of complaints, but it is worthy of our humanity to look into the long mirrors of history with our fists clenched fiercely at our side, our minds scanning time as death continues to play tag with little children, leaving nothing behind but their shadows. Such poetry gives us truths and tunes to hum while walking past endless graveyards.

Ingesting Violence as Witness

WHAT WE MEAN BY POETRY OF WITNESS IS DEFINED BY MASS violence in the way of torture, battle, massacre, and genocide. It is broad and it is deep, especially when the poetry ingests violence in a complex or layered way, managing to speak from within the vise of history and trauma.

Poetry of witness deals with pain of the body and mind, often in self-conscious ways. But being self-conscious does not negate the imperative of poetic form—as in the cases of Walt Whitman, Wilfred Owen, Paul Celan, Primo Levi, Anna Akhmatova, Zbigniew Herbert, Mahmoud Darwish, or Peter Balakian, for example.

Such poetry is uncomfortable to those who prefer an academically shaped genteel sensibility. The opponents of poetry of witness denounce it as a politicization of poetry, a bald moral accounting, or an overly-emotional recounting of history. These opponents overlook the relationship between poetry and trauma, and the fact that we all live in the shadow of history.

Poetry of witness is a major resistance to the virtually inevitable fact of forgetting. *Lest We Forget, We Must Never Forget, Remember Me, Memento Mori*: these are some of its persistent mottos.

Poetry of witness is post-memory—especially if it

emanates from a writer who may be born after the memorialized event. The trauma and the poetry make the connection between the poet and the event after (often long after) the event.

Poetry Survives the Ages

CAROLYN FORCHÉ (AMERICAN POET AND ANTHOLOGIST) once went to El Salvador, knowing that a civil war was coming. She felt uncomfortable revealing that she was a poet because she thought it was much more important in the context of poverty and oppression to be a doctor or a human rights lawyer or even, perhaps, a journalist. She was surprised at the positive reaction she received.

Why? she wondered. She was told by a Salvadoran friend that it had nothing to do with ideology, but everything to do with involvement—her understanding of the political situation on a level quite different from sheer politics or sociology. As a poet, her reaction was direct and under no illusion of objectivity. Her voice would rise above the cacophony of loud political voices, above polemics. Moreover, she was informed by the Salvadoran, it was because of the *essential* language of poetry.

Forché's reflections on the issue are enlightening. Given the extreme politics of the situation, it was inevitable that politics would enter into her poetry—at least as language, though not as doctrine. Salvadoran poetry at the time was poetry of news—as it probably is in any part of the world where poverty, oppression, and desperation are defining qualities of life. "It's also because it's in the surround," Forché asserts, offering an illustration of New England poetry of nature—where a seasonal world would prompt a poet to notice such things as snow, geese migrations, and bitter winds. And so, this world enters the poet's awareness and sensibility.

When a poem takes a true measure of a terrible event, it can make the age grimace in fear at the power of the printed word. This means, of course, that the poem at its most basic level is real news because it brings to light something that runs counter to the dominant thinking of the place and period. And some societies cannot bear to have such news. It's true, as Stanley Kunitz once remarked, that to live as a poet in an oppressive society is "the aesthetic equivalent of a major political statement." Sometimes commissars take violent action against the poet. But great poetry, like all great art, has an after-life.

Forché puts into evidence Walt Whitman's poems about nursing soldiers during the Civil War, to which I (and she) could add Osip Mandelstam's *Voronezh Notebooks*, Anna Akhmatova's *Requiem* about the Stalinist terror, Yevgeny Yevtushenko's *Babiy Yar*, Yusef Komunyakaa's Vietnam poems, Yeats' poetry about Ireland, and poems by Paul Celan, Czeslaw Milosz, Zbigniew Herbert, Mahmoud Darwish, Wislawa Szymborska, Charles Simic, *et cetera*.

Such poetry shows an essential language and unique awareness about context, surviving to become something greater than its context.

Out of the scattered debris of politics and history emerge many voices that echo what Emmanuel Levinas called "our infinite and inexhaustible responsibility to the other."

Armenian Poetry

As with Israeli or Palestinian poetry, Armenian poetry shows clearly and sometimes crudely the pressure of history and culture—the centuries of ancient empire, the horror of the genocide and its denial by the Turks, the sorry economic and political plight of present-day Armenians in their homeland, and (in the case of those who retain their religious faith) Biblical resonances. To borrow an apt image from M.L. Rosenthal, it's as if history leaps "from the poem's fingertips to the nerve-ends" of readers.

Tragedy is an ever-present undercurrent rather like Saroyan's grief under his human comedy. And fear or terror has an almost pathological quality because Armenians (wherever they've settled) live with a tenacious memory of annihilation or near-annihilation. The poetry touches the nerves of searing historical memory and chagrin.

The colours of Armenian poetry are pigments of bitter consciousness.

There was will and there was a wanting. The most talented of their generation wrote blazingly between 1909 and 1915 and then their lives were snuffed out. They all willed an indigenous literature—one in an array of distinctive styles that would serve as witness to history, and they all wanted to live, to savour the pleasures of life rather than the abstract glory of martyrdom.

Their poems did not invent worlds. There was no need for this. They had a small world that was in immediate danger of being obliterated, and their poetry would mirror the awfulness of the human face, heart, and hand.

But the greatest Armenian poetry makes singing poetry out of the materials of disaster. And the spiritual resources that energize and support this melodic urge create a poise in the face of history's savage blows.

How Armenian Poetry
is Different from Canadian

ITS LANGUAGE IS MADE BY CARAVANS OF FEET.
The air can be claustrophobic.
History lies like ash on its tongue.
One cannot wish away the disasters.
Tragedy is daily fare, and there are numerous connoisseurs.
The head of Siamanto hangs out of a metaphoric tree.

Volatile Elements of Poetry

Ce

"Terribly far away I saw your mouth in the wild light:
it seemed to me you were shouting instructions to us all."

THESE LINES BY ADRIENNE RICH ON IMAMU AMIRI BARAKA
(LeRoi Jones) recognize the modern inferno of Black Lives—
not the movement but the collective tribe. The nightmare
world has a voice that wildly shouts instructions, reawaken-
ing consciousness of social or political revolution.

We're confronted in the work of Baraka and that of
other militant poets by the use of political consciousness as
a volatile element of poetics.

Of course, it wasn't just black poets who revealed the
power of such a volatile element. Before Baraka there was
certainly Ezra Pound, and before him William Butler Yeats,
and before him ...

All these poets had great audiences.

Their Canadian counterparts—Klein, Layton,
Acorn—had to fight for theirs. Klein went silent much too
early. Layton became increasingly strident, almost hysterical about politics when overtaken by his own volatility.
And Acorn died a troubled man.

Are there contemporary audiences for contemporary
volatile poetry? Or has such poetry become the domain of
the colourful eccentric, the self-evident propagandist, the
narcissistic media whore, the false prophet?

Indigiqueer Poets

FIRST NATIONS QUEER MALE POETS BARE THEIR WOUNDS IN their indigenous worlds. Four of them move through dark worlds of childhood and manhood with language that is intense, furious, raw, lyrical, incantatory. Gregory Scofield is Metis "hip," moving from boyhood whimpers to inconsolable howls. Jordan Abel drives his deconstructive cleverness through racist texts, erasing sentences colonially constructed, forging a concrete space with confrontational inversions. Joshua Whitehead creates a trickster persona to re-centre his Two-Spirit, literary, cyberpunk identity. And Billy-Ray Belcourt has a breath-taking boldness and intellectual acumen, rupturing attachments, succumbing to instability, working towards a poetics of the "unbodied."

Their bodies (in Billy-Ray's sharp perception) "don't always feel like bodies but like wounds." And these wounds make them post-modern warriors, battling against the "semiotics of indigeneity" that routes them into "death worlds." Hear them sing like astonishing ghosts intervening in present-day harrowing life. Their songs are the most honest, most cutting, most fully engaged lyrics and anti-lyrics in the land.

These poets create songs of emptiness, absences, contaminations, and transformations with sheer candour, bemused forms, agile lexicons, and layered precisions. But literary ratiocinations are, perhaps, misleading. All these poets have minds and hearts on fire, not mere exotic campfires or *literary* conflagrations.

Poetry and Persian Wrestling

Marcello Di Cintio's book *Poets & Pahlevans* (2006) reveals a little of the paradoxical history of poetry and wrestling. Having been a wrestler himself before turning to travel writing and creative non-fiction, Di Cintio undertakes a journey into the heart of Iran to give us palpable evidence of how the two seemingly disconnected activities flourish in Persian culture.

Among the many fascinating pieces of information are the following:

All Iranians, even small children, can recite poetry from memory.

Poets who have been dead for centuries are revered.

Ferdosi's 11th century epic poem *Shahnomeh* (Book of Kings) (with which I was familiar as a schoolboy in Bombay) recalls a thousand years of Persian history and has as its central hero, a Hercules-like warrior named Rostam (or Rustom), the "archetypal pahlevan," who kills his rival Sohrab in battle, only to discover that the man was his son. There are paintings on Iranian tea-house walls and restaurants of Rostam, clad in battle armour and weeping over the body of Sohrab.

Early in this national poetic treasure, the monster Ghu leads a demon army into battle against Persia. King Tahumers and his brave force of soldiers defeat the demons in a pitched battle, during which the king dashes the monster's brains out with a single stroke of his mace. The demon army falls but begs to be spared from execution. Its warriors vow that they will teach the Persians something wonderful, bringing the king a box of books, pens, and ink, and teaching him the art of the word. Di Cintio sums it up succinctly: "Through the muscles of men, a warrior's mercy and the gift of demons, the poets of Persia were born."

Omar Khayyam's *Rubaiyat* (in English poet Edward Fitzgerald's translation) is world-famous, even though the English translation is not a faithful one. In fact, Fitzgerald is remembered for his rendering of Khayyam's verse rather than his own. I own a tattered paperback copy (from my teenage years) with elegant black and white line drawings.

Farid al-Din Attar, though not as internationally famous as Khayyam, is more revered in Iran than Khayyam. His name suggests he was a perfumer or apothecary, "responsible for distilling the attar of flowers and herbs into fragrance and remedy." He eventually gave up his store to travel with a group of mystics, journeying to Mecca, Damascus, and India, where he studied with a Sufi order. Attar's masterwork is the "Conference of the Birds," an allegorical search for God in the Sufi mystic tradition.

But what of wrestling specifically and poetry?

The connection is made from the outset in the first chapter. An old man recites poetry into a microphone, broadcasting measured verses through a static-garbled loudspeaker. When the poem ends, he summons two barefooted wrestlers to the centre of a circle. The grapplers brush the ground with their fingertips before touching their lips and forehead in an invocation to Allah. The wrestlers shake hands, kiss each other on both cheeks, then lock their arms around each other as the official start of the contest, further sanctioned by the referee's tap on their shoulders.

The preliminary rituals denote a form of civility—a word that Di Cintio claims is "old-fashioned and is rarely used any more, but lingers in the memories of men like the perfect world of poetry and the skills of old wrestlers."

Wrestling has its own ancient rituals but it derives inspiration from poetry.

PART THREE

ON THEORY
AND PRACTICE

"Schools" of Poetry

When I participated in a reading/symposium with Creative Writing students at the University of Toronto Erindale campus, I had to field a number of questions about schools of poetry. Did I belong to one, and if so which one and for what reason? What did I think of schools of poetry? The aspiring young writers were quite genuinely surprised (perhaps secretly scandalized?) when I expressed my extreme aversion to the very idea of a school of poetry—or a school of any type of writing. I quietly reminded them that Shakespeare didn't belong to any such school; neither did Keats, nor any of the great modern poets I admired. I further suggested that a school of poetry—as distinguished from a course in writing—could actually harm a writer because a school is founded on a specific ideology, set of values, and biases. In other words, its own propaganda because each school is exclusive unto itself.

Stephen Burt writes the following in his stimulating book *Close Calls with Nonsense (Reading New Poetry)*: "As with rock and roll, the names for trends and schools now fifteen years old have limited use when applied to the art being made now. Yet it's surprisingly hard to discuss contemporary poetry without naming camps and schools: sometimes, people won't let you."

A stunning admission and a sad one for poetry.

I abhor schools of poetry. I only familiarize myself with them as one of my duties as a literary critic—so that I can tell the differences among the multiple schools and, therefore, their fraternities or sororities—and so that I can decode, decipher, and describe what the poems say or appear to say.

My bias is motivated by my belief that craft and art, like life, is capacious and more complicated that any poet's version of it.

Mouthful of Words, of Breath

YEATS ONCE BOASTED OF A POEM: "I MADE IT OUT OF A mouthful of air." And he wasn't being precious or affected. He was merely iterating what every poet does—at least, every poet who believes with Edward Hirsch that poetry is "a voicing, a calling forth, and the lyric poem exists somewhere in the region—the register—between speech and song."

When I write a poem, I don't think of spatial organization at first—of how it will look as an arrangement in verse or line break. I first sound it out in my head and audibly in my mouth. When I recite it, the act of mouthing the words is a form of entering into an intimacy with the language and my own interiority—as well as with an audience of one or more outside my self.

Hirsch contrasts the New Testament idea that "In the beginning was the Word" with Martin Buber's claim in *I and Thou* that "In the beginning is the relation." It may be simply a distinction without a difference, for it is the word that forges a relationship between poet and thought, poet and image, poet and audience. And shouldn't a poet love the word or its sound as a primal pleasure?

Can There Be Poetry
after Donald Trump?

ℯ

READING GEORGE STEINER'S RESPONSE TO ADORNO'S NIHILISM caused me to ponder a latter-day obscenity: Donald Trump's "thugging" his way to the American Presidency, normalizing mendacity, narcissism, misogyny, corruption, child abuse, racism, international terrorism, sub-literacy, and mass hallucination. The vision of this least educated, least trustworthy, most inept American president ever (disgraced even further by his choice of woefully atrocious cabinet members and White House staff) prompts the question: Can there be poetry after Trump? Or will literacy be reduced to Trumpism, i.e. a string of short brain farts masquerading as ideas and delivered in three-or-four-word-phrases (many misspelled and ungrammatical), repeated at least three times, in case the Trumpster (adult) or Trumpite (minor) forget what each fart was supposed to mean?

Derridean Clones

Ơ

DERRIDEAN LITERARY THEORY ADVOCATES RELATIVITY.

But with terms such as "begin," "key," "unravel," and "dominant," is the subject helplessly clouded?

If there is no real origin of a text, can there be a beginning?

If there is no true centre but only margins, can there be "key" words or a dominant discourse other than those of the critic's making?

The essence of the Deconstructive critic is arrogance.

The arrogance of one who deliberately reads against an author's clearest intention.

The arrogance of assuming that an author is unreliable and may even be absent from what he writes.

The arrogance of being against closure ... all the while assuming that the critic, unlike the author, is really present and not absent, and that his own taxonomic system is reliable.

How Postmodern
Poetry Moves

An opening gambit should confuse,
(perhaps) potential romanticism
morphing into tonal misdirection,
compelling a reader to hold endless
possibilities in suspension.
Infinitude of anxiety.
Waiting to see where the poem
eventually goes, if it isn't simply
spinning wheels in the suspended mind.

The second stanza shouldn't help much,
only introduce a more elaborate metaphor
with vague signification, say, raising sails
when floating inside an empty bottle.
Before the poet clarifies the structure,
best to bounce off various interpretations,
like an action painter tossing paints
at a blank canvas, or, perhaps, (like)
a precocious chimp with oils and a gift
for colour, or an elephant using his phallic trunk.

Such major pleasure could add to confusion,
of course, tilt the poem completely off-balance,
but if you can't find the axis, would it matter?
(And do you notice how I employ parenthesis?
Cunning poetic ploy for claptrap applause.)

Private meaning should be esoteric,
the poem use only the tense of a feeling,
non-gendered for greater ambiguity
and more exciting guesswork.
Now we have only images and impressions—
perfect for a scholarly plot of changing grammar,
tense, and syntax. Ominous connotations
which, ideally, return you to the start
of what began your confusion, without
necessarily clearing it up. Bravo!

The Hatred of Poetry[1]

MARIANNE MOORE GAVE RISE TO THE ASSUMPTION THAT poetry is generally hated when she wrote:

> I, too, dislike it.
> Reading it, however, with a perfect
> contempt for it, one discovers in
> it, after all, a place for the genuine.

Her four lines, however, are hardly demonstrative of a contempt for poetry, which Ben Lerner appears to have. Lerner's long essay (short book), entitled *The Hatred of Poetry*, is an extended "negative rumination" before it attempts to be "a kind of manic, mantric affirmation" that he thinks is close to "unceasing prayer." Well, one man's mantra is another's insanity.

Lerner's essay raises more flags than a UN assembly and to far less positive effect. It creates tautology after tautology more often than a Jesuitical apologia for God: for example, his use of such phrases as "actual poem, the genuine article" that mean nothing specific (for what is "actual" or "genuine" in a poem formally?) and yet function as buzz words in his peculiar attack on lyric poetry.

---

1. This essay owes its genesis to my book review of Ben Lerner's *The Hatred of Poetry* originally published in *World Literature Today*, January 2017.

Whether making reference to Caedmon ("the first poet in English whose name we know"), Allan Grossman (Lerner's ideal critic), or others, Lerner's assumptions about poetry are perversely utopian because they needlessly posit an ideal that can never be achieved. Using a lot of learned lumber and a great deal of corny, contrived examples, he accuses poetry of not possessing a quality that he claims is impossible to possess. To summarize his argument: poetry arises from a desire to reach the transcendent and divine by going beyond the finite and the historical. This can't be done. So, a poet is "a tragic figure" and any poem is "always a record of failure." Indeed, you can only compose poems that make a place for the genuine that never appears.

As a perceptive reviewer countered, this is like complaining about not having been visited by Santa Claus, while simultaneously claiming that he isn't real in the first place.

Moreover, if Lerner is correct about poetry, he must also necessarily be correct about dance, acting, painting, sculpture, the novel, the short story—indeed, any human art or craft that must be measured against a tautological ideal.

And why is this a big deal? Anyone who has studied philosophy knows that the ideal can never be achieved in practice, but this hardly justifies contempt or hatred. Not to admit such a self-evident truth would turn the Lerner poets of this world into self-hating poseurs, burdened by the weight of their own rhetorical strategies meant to argue against themselves in the chance echo of a possible poem.

What Story
Does Poetry Tell?

$\mathcal{Q}$

In his essay "Shakespeare The Poet," Anthony Burgess points out that the whole concept of poetry on which Shakespeare's *Venus and Adonis* was based is different from our own in the 20th century. "You took a narrative theme in those days and a set verse form and then you went to work, wondering what lyric sparks would be struck from the flint of laborious engagement. Nowadays poetry has become almost totally egocentric and it is not expected to tell a story."

I don't necessarily share Burgess' implicit admiration of approaching poetry like a laboratory experiment, but he has a point about the tendency of modern poetry to avoid telling a story—outside the explicitly narrative form. There are justly famous long poems, as well as anthologies devoted to these, but I think that Burgess' larger point is that the modern lyric or even the modern anti-lyric eschews the personality of the creator. "Indeed, we are told to think of art as creating itself," declares Burgess. And, of course, we know better: art never creates itself, even though creation springs from the subconscious.

Little wonder that I'm more interested in poets who reveal human nature and who clarify what this could be.

What, for instance, did Neruda, the eponymous character in Pablo Larrain's 2016 film, mean by his admission:

"Tonight I can write the saddest lines ..." In the film's narrative, he's on the run from the law because of his political beliefs. But that line has other resonances in context.

Neruda's line is a ghost of some private reality.

Would a contemporary editor ask him to delete such a line because of its candid emotionality?

When You Explain It, Poetry Becomes Banal

IN MICHAEL RADFORD'S CHARMING FILM, *IL POSTINO* (1994), Mario Ruoppolo is a rather emaciated postman who delivers mail on bicycle to celebrated Chilean poet Pablo Neruda exiled in Italy. Mario is charmed by Neruda's love poems, but is baffled by the line "the smell of barber shops makes me sob." "Why?" he asks Neruda. "When you explain it, poetry becomes banal," the poet asserts, maintaining that better than any explanation is the expression of feelings.

Is Neruda's answer too simple? Is it an excuse to avoid clarity?

But some feelings are too deep for explanation. Not the feeling in Wordsworth's "Daffodils" or the feeling in Frost's "On Stopping by the Woods on a Snowy Evening." Not even the feeling in most English sonnets. Or the feeling in Mario Ruoppolo's metaphor about his beloved Beatrice's smile that spreads like a butterfly.

How about some feelings in particular poems where form and content are perfectly congruent, when punctuation establishes a score, when emotion is channelled suavely by diction?

Sometimes explication and dissection can murder art. You have only to read pretentious academic theories and analyses of poetry to realize this fact.

This is not to make a case against interpretation, however. It is simply to acknowledge that a yearning for floodlight explicitness contradicts the impulse and motive for poetry.

Poetry is on the
Side of Humanists

MARIO RUOPPOLO IN *IL POSTINO* IS NOT REPRESENTATIVE OF your everyday postman. How many postmen do we know who are familiar with Dante or have a beloved named Beatrice? He doesn't even know what a metaphor is, until Pablo Neruda enlightens him. And then he can't seem to stop himself from creating waves of metaphors, turning himself into a boat tossing on waves of figurative speech. Innocent that he is, he associates poetry with love, charmed by the fact that Neruda and his wife address each other as *amor*. And one of his prime motives in learning how to read and write poetry is to acquire a means to make women fall for him and to woo his Beatrice.

Many a poet has demonstrated a similar motive.

But one special thing Mario learns is that Neruda isn't simply the poet of love, but the poet of the people. A crucially important distinction.

Canada has the Milton Acorn Prize, nominally awarded to a people's poet, though in recent decades the prize seems to have gone to academic poets who are the farthest thing from people's poets. Their poetry tends towards the cerebrally abstract, the esoterically narcotic, the triumphantly deconstructive—the very contrary of what humanism implies.

Even Baudelaire Wrote B.S.

STEPHEN DOBYNS ARGUES IN *NEXT WORD, BETTER WORD* *(The Craft of Writing Poetry)*, that literary art (especially poetry) doesn't have a moral agenda, though it can have a moral function. He puts into play this quotation from Baudelaire:

> Poetry has no other aim or object but herself; she can have no other ... I am not attempting to say that poetry does not ennoble morals—please understand me aright—or that its final result is not to lift man up above the level of vulgar interests ... I am simply saying that if a poet pursues a moral aim, he will have weakened his poetic powers and it would not be rash to wager that the result will be a bad work ... and when an exquisite poem melts us into tears, those tears are not the proof of an excess of pleasure, but rather evidence of a certain petulant, impatient sorrow—of a nervous postulation—of a nature exiled amid the imperfect ... Thus the Poetic Principle lies, strictly and simply, in human aspiration toward a supernal Beauty, and the manifestation of that principle in an enthusiasm of the soul—an enthusiasm entirely independent of Passion, which is the intoxication of the heart, and of Truth which is the grazing ground of reason.

There are so many flaws in this assertion, it's hard to know where to begin. For one thing, any literary art must have an aim beyond itself, or it is relegated to the level of pure aestheticism, which is fine if you want the primary purpose of art to be the creation of a cold museum-piece, perfectly wrought, that can be admired behind protective glass. (This, alas, has become a prevailing practice in Canada by our academic poets who have, for the most part, lost contact with human emotion in their chaste dedication to technique and pretentiousness.) It's hard to know what Baudelaire means by "a moral aim." Is it moral rehabilitation, transformation of society, education reform, religious prescription, civic reform, or some other special aim? Poetic powers can be weakened by a number of things—such as false dichotomies, anomalies of diction, weak metrical rhythm, inconsistent tone, adjectival hypertrophy, *et cetera*—so, emotion or passion is hardly an essential flaw. Baudelaire seems to be blissfully unaware of his own weird contradiction when he castigates an "exquisite poem" for melting us into tears. Perhaps he is merely being ironic, but I suspect he truly believes—as, apparently, many of our leading academic poets do—that literary art must be objective, technically perfect, and not given so easily to feeling—merely to the imitation or representation of that feeling.

Baudelaire gives himself completely away when he writes about poetry aspiring to "supernal beauty." If he did, indeed, understand the meaning of his adjective, he would surely see that he has his head in the clouds ("supernal" relates to the heavens), no matter where his feet are placed. But he compounds the problem by yoking together "enthusiasm" (as distinct from passion) and "soul"—an action that qualifies him admirably for some religious ministry, perhaps in a sort of poetic Vatican. If it does nothing else, his argument redounds on itself, for it shows how his moral effect is really the result of a moral agenda.

What William Carlos Williams Meant

CONTEMPORARY POETRY HAS BECOME INCREASINGLY confused about its own range and efficacy. It often seems to reject an emphasis on voice, in the perverse view that such an emphasis is old-fashioned. In so doing, it gets many things wrong about the dynamics of voice, as well as the dynamics of poetry.

There is another perverse notion in contemporary poetry—though it seems to be more prevalent in Canada than in the U.S. This one concerns a misunderstanding of William Carlos Williams' dictum "No ideas but in things." It's a skewed interpretation because (as Frank Bidart puts it) Williams never said just "no ideas."

Moreover, it is simplistic to reject ideas as being anti-poetic because (as Bidart illustrates) there are great poets whose lines often eschew the image in favour of a philosophical idea or concept, as in Ezra Pound. But why limit oneself to Pound? One could point to Jorie Graham, Bidart himself, Michael Palmer, or even Emily Dickinson as in this instance:

> Behind Me—dips Eternity—
> Before Me—Immortality—
> Myself—the Term between—

This is not to imply that such poetry is image-free. It's simply to make a case for abstraction in poetry. Abstraction that doesn't necessarily smother feeling in a poem. As Bidart notes: "reaching for abstractions and conceiving abstractions are not separable from feeling for a human being." And he could point to his superb "Poem Ending with a Sentence by Heath Ledger" as characteristic of his own writing, where the quoted sentence is part of a clever patterning of lines in sequence ("a single line followed by a two-line stanza, followed by another single line followed by a two-line stanza"). The pattern becomes a hook for his idea *and* feeling.

Cultural Appropriation

℘

THE *NEW YORK TIMES* REPORTS: "BRISBANE, AUSTRALIA—
Officials in charge of a writers' festival in Australia were so
upset with the address by their keynote speaker, the American novelist Lionel Shriver, that they censored her on the
festival website and publicly disavowed her remarks."

The hurriedly organized "Right of Reply" by her critics
further roiled the festival. There were imputations of colonial arrogance, runaway political incorrectness, and un-
fettered exploitation of the experiences of others. The usual
knee-jerk or high-dudgeon reactions by writers who should
know better: writing is not bureaucracy for commissars.
Nor is it a Global Treaty Organization with sharp boundaries and No Man's Land.

A writer is free to appropriate any persona or point of
view he wishes. The only test is the quality of the writing. In
other words, is the writing true to life and true for the chan-
nels of narrative? Does it bring its characters credibly to life?
Does it provide new insight into techniques of cultural ap-
propriation?

Good thing that Shakespeare wasn't part of the Brisbane Writers Festival. He would have found himself excoriated and excommunicated for appropriating a French saint,
a Jewish Venetian moneylender, a Moor proud of his racial
intermarriage, Italian adolescents with raging hormones,

Romans, Greeks, Persians, Spaniards, Italian cardinals, French kings and dauphins, a prince of Morocco, *et cetera*.

To be in accord with the writers of this festival, Shakespeare would have had to limit himself to the point of view of a middle-aged English burgher turned playwright of Elizabethan propaganda about the Divine Right of Kings and the Great Chain of Being.

Or, perhaps, he would have been decreed to write about the manufacture of gloves (his father was a glover) or about "shotgun" weddings. (Anne Hathaway was eight years older than him and was with child when he married her.) Or, perhaps, about the Elizabethan school system with a supplementary recommendation for pedagogic and scholastic improvements.

How Long Does It Take to Write a Book?

$\mathcal{C}$

IT DEPENDS ON THE GENRE AND THE SUBJECT. A PROSE biography takes a few years, including the background research, interviews, and drafts. Poetry can be different, but again much depends on the subject and the forms used.

Poetry is perhaps the most dependent on spontaneous inspiration. But what is meant by inspiration? Is it a sudden flash of an image, a word, a phrase? Or is it a sudden propulsion to create after one has been inspired by a fellow or superior writer? Is it this unexpected but thrilling stimulation of the mind and senses?

I like to think of a book shaped by themes and my driven need to express them in images and rhythmic units of thought and feeling. I'm not one who simply writes disparate poems, allowing them to accumulate over time and reveal thematic or stylistic links. This isn't to disparage other poets who work this way. I elect to write a full book. In other words, I elect to complete a long project with its own unique form. Each poem has its own specific form and problems, but the idea of a unified book sets the work in motion. I already have some sort of context, a range of tones and moods.

Annie Dillard proclaims in *The Writing Life*: "Writing every book, the writer must solve two problems: Can it be done? and, Can I do it?"

My answers are always in the affirmative—even with

the recognition that there are going to be defects. Measured by standards of perfection, every book fails to some degree. But, like Samuel Beckett, we keep failing but each time we can hopefully fail better and better.

The writer's first duty is to himself. He is himself his own first audience, a silent one who listens intently to the quiet work of filling a blank sheet of paper with words, phrases, and lines that will keep his first excitement alive and growing.

Writing Poems with a
Book Structure in Mind

Many, if not most, poets write "stand-alone" or independent lyrics or poems that aren't necessarily related to a full-length manuscript. But is it better to simply have a book that is a gathering together of such independent poems or to write poems with a book structure in mind?

Many poems start from an emotional impulse in the poet, and then the writer has to find different formal strategies to develop that emotional engagement. Such poems, when they come into being, may not have any thematic, stylistic, or emotional links. They could be the result of poetic philandering—a case of moving from one genre or sub-genre to another, one theme to another. Very often in the writing process, however, the poems could evolve as a sequence of an idea or feeling—or as functioning parts of some structure such as a society or tribe or landscape or tradition or language. Poems are an act of discovery, and the discovery could well be a matter of following and extending an impulse experienced by the first poem. In other words, when the impulse is experienced, it could generate a successive impulse, and that one a third, and so forth, helping bring a sequence into being.

In the case of a book-length structure, the dynamic of creativity is different. First, such a structure is really akin to a long poem made up of sections or sequences or themes.

You can gain something by combining poems rather than having them stand on their own. And you can gain even more by not simply collecting disparate poems and finding a way to combine them under an umbrella, as such, but by an overarching movement or progression. There is also more of the feeling of a narrative, not necessarily in a literal sense, of course, but as an overall story that emerges from individual poems.

You can think of book-length structure in terms of montage, that cinematic term for assembling, structuring, linking together images that aren't necessarily readily associated as an organic grouping.

So, a poet could make an entire book of poetry from ...

a pattern of imagery
a single narrative voice
a patterning of inwardness
an interplay of voices
various poetic genres linked to a theme
an interplay of lyric and anti-lyric
a philosophical argument
a biography
autobiography.

A book of collected "stand-alone" poems and a book of poems written specifically to be linked in a unified structure both share the same question and mystery of closure.

How does a poet know when to end the book? At what moment does it become clear to him that he doesn't need another poem for the book because the structure is sound, and that another element might make it wobble or tilt perilously to the point of collapse?

In one sense the matter of closure is a pragmatic question. In another, it's a mystery because closure can be simply guesswork or intuition and not based on any absolute assurance.

And at this point in this book, I can follow Omar Khayyam and write: *Tamam shud* (Ended).

About the Author

Keith Garebian has been writing professionally about theatre since 1976 for numerous magazines, journals, tabloids, and anthologies. Winner of a Canada Council Senior Grant (to complete an authoritative biography of William Hutt), numerous grants from the Ontario Arts Council, and four Mississauga Arts Council Awards for Established Writing, he has served on writing and theatre juries for the OAC. His production histories of classic Broadway musicals culminated in *The Making of 'Cabaret'* (rev. and expanded ed.) (Oxford University Press). His reputation as a theatre scholar is further extended by his massive biography, *William Hutt: Soldier Actor* (Guernica), and *Colours to the Chameleon: Canadian Actors on Shakespeare* (Guernica).

Although he turned to poetry relatively late in his career, Garebian has produced eight poetry collections in the last 16 years, including *Frida: Paint Me as a Volcano* (Buschek), *Blue: The Derek Jarman Poems* (Signature Editions), *Children of Ararat* (Frontenac), *Poetry is Blood* (Guernica), and the autobiographical *Against Forgetting* (Frontenac). Many of his poems have been translated into French, Armenian, Romanian, and Bulgarian. One of his Derek Jarman poems (alongside a poem each by Thomas Merton and Denise Levertov) was set to music for choir and instruments by celebrated

American composer Gregory Spears, debuting (under the umbrella title "The Tower and the Garden") in 2018 in Philadelphia and San Francisco, prior to a New York premiere in 2019.

In 2013 Keith Garebian was awarded the William Saroyan Medal by the Republic of Armenia for his writing and work on behalf of the Armenian Diaspora.

This book is made of paper from well-managed FSC® - certified forests, recycled materials, and other controlled sources.

 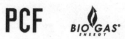